BASIC POLICY STUDIES SKILLS

Edited by:

William D. Coplin
Michael K. O'Leary

With assistance from:

Renee S. Captor
Tammy J. Kissell

P. O. Box 337
Croton-on-Hudson, N.Y. 10520

Copyright (c) 1981 by William D. Coplin and Michael K. O'Leary
Syracuse University

ISBN 0 936826 14 2

Policy Studies Associates was established in 1976 to strengthen
learning resources in order to help students develop policy analysis
skills and techniques and apply these to important public issues.
Toward this end, two series of learning packages have been published,
designed especially for undergraduate use -- Policy Sciences Series,
which emphasizes techniques in policy analysis, and Policy Issues
Series, which concentrates on specific public policy questions.

An operating program of the Council on International and Public
Affairs, Policy Studies Associates is a cooperative nonprofit undertaking of a small group of faculty members and others concerned with
improving the quality of education on public policy issues in schools,
colleges, and universities.

TABLE OF CONTENTS

LISTING OF DISPLAYS ix

INTRODUCTION: A FRAMEWORK FOR STUDY xi

CHAPTER ONE: ANALYZING PUBLIC POLICY ISSUES 1

   I. Organizing Information on Public Policy Issues 2

      A. The Basic Framework: Environment, Actors,
           Policies 3

      B. Summary 5

      Exercise 1.1: Applying the Framework to a
                  Public Policy Issue 6

  II. Organizing Values on Public Policy Issues 7

      A. Self-interest Values 8

      B. Public Interest Values 9

      Optional Exercise: The Good Society Exercise 12

      C. Values in the Analysis of Public Policy
           Issues 13

      Exercise 1.2: Value Analysis 14

III. Types of Public Policy Analysis -- Monitoring,
      Forecasting, Evaluation, and Prescription 15

      A. Monitoring 16

      B. Forecasting 19

      C. Evaluation 27

      D. Prescription 32

      Exercise 1.3: Applying the Four Types of
      Analysis 35

      Appendix I: Rules for the Good Society Exercise ... 36

CHAPTER TWO: LIBRARY RESEARCH FOR THE ANALYSIS OF
              PUBLIC POLICY 40

   I. Introduction 41

       Exercise 2.1: Choosing a Topic 41

  II. Definitions -- Dictionaries and Encyclopedias 42

       Exercise 2.2: Dictionaries and Encyclopedias 44

 III. Background Information -- Journal Articles 45

       Exercise 2.3: Finding Journal Articles 48

  IV. Descriptions of Conditions -- Almanacs, Yearbooks,
       and Statistical Sources 49

       Exercise 2.4: Finding Statistics 50

   V. Events -- Newspapers and Surveys of Events 52

       Exercise 2.5: Finding Events 53

  VI. Information Through Documents -- U.S.
       Government Publications 54

       Exercise 2.6a: Finding Government Documents 57

       Exercise 2.6b: Using Census Data 59

 VII. Information Tool -- Using Microforms 60

       Exercise 2.7: Microforms 61

VIII.   In-depth Information -- Locating Books 62

        Exercise 2.8: Books 64

  IX.   The Legal Side -- Using the Law Library 66

        A.   Legal Dictionaries 66

        Exercise 2.9a: Legal Dictionaries 66

        B.   Legal Periodicals 67

        Exercise 2.9b: Legal Periodicals 67

        C.   Statutes 68

        Exercise 2.9c: Finding Statutes 68

        D.   U.S. Supreme Court Cases 68

        Exercise 2.9d: Locating Supreme Court Cases 69

        E.   Administrative Regulations 70

        Exercise 2.9e: Locating Regulations 70

   X.   The Final Resource -- Using Bibliographies 71

        Exercise 2.10: Using Bibliographies 71

CHAPTER THREE: INTRODUCTION TO SURVEYS AND INTERVIEWS 73

   I.   Introduction to Surveys 74

  II.   Designing a Sample Survey 76

        Exercise 3.1:   Research Objectives for a Sample
        Survey 79

 III.   Target Population 80

        Exercise 3.2: Target Population 81

  IV.   Types of Sampling Procedures 82

        A.   Nonrandom Sampling Procedures 82

        B.   Random Sampling 83

        C.   Conclusions 85

        Exercise 3.3: Sampling Procedures 85

V. Information-gathering Techniques and Types of
    Responses 86

    A. Information-gathering Techniques 86

    B. Open-ended and Closed Responses 87

    Exercise 3.4: Information-gathering Techniques 89

    Exercise 3.5: Types of Responses 89

    C. Bias in the Sample Survey 90

    Exercise 3.6: Bias and Other Problems 91

CHAPTER FOUR: DESCRIPTIVE STATISTICS FOR PUBLIC POLICY
               ANALYSIS 92

I. Presentation of Statistical Data 93

    A. Tabular Methods 93

    B. Data Documentation 96

    C. Levels of Measurement 97

    Exercise 4.1: Tabular Methods 100

II. Graphic Methods of Data Display 101

    A. Basic Graphing Skills 101

    B. Types of Graphs 103

    Exercise 4.2: Bar Graphs, Trend Lines, and
                   Pie Charts 107

III. Mean and Standard Deviation 108

    A. The Mean 108

    B. The Standard Deviation 110

    Exercise 4.3: Mean and Standard Deviation 112

IV. Measures of Association -- Nominal Data 113

    A. Contingency Table 114

    B. Yule's Q 117

    Exercise 4.4: Contingency Table and Yule's Q 119

V. Measures of Association -- Interval and Ratio
    Data 120

    A. The Scatterplot 120

    B. Pearson's r -- The Pearson Product-moment
        Correlation Coefficient 124

    Exercise 4.5: Scatterplot and Pearson's r 127

CHAPTER FIVE: POLICY EVALUATION 128

    I. An Introduction to the Use of Benefits and Costs
        of Public Policy 129

    A. Defining Benefits and Costs 129

    B. An Informal Application of Some Benefit-Cost
        Concepts 130

    C. Classifying Benefits and Costs 131

    Exercise 5.1: Benefits and Costs 132

   II. The Need for Research Design 133

    Exercise 5.2: Benefits and Costs in Evaluation 134

  III. Some Basic Concepts Necessary to Understand
        Types of Research Designs 135

    A. Definitions 135

    Exercise 5.3: Applying the Definitions 137

   IV. Research Designs 138

    A. Pre-experimental Designs 138

    B. True-experimental Designs 141

    C. Quasi-experimental Designs 144

    Exercise 5.4: Identifying Designs................. 147

    Exercise 5.5: Research Designs 153

    V. The Question of Validity 154

    Exercise 5.6: Validity 156

CHAPTER SIX: ANALYZING POLITICS WITH THE PRINCE POLITICAL
ACCOUNTING SYSTEM 157

  I.   Introduction 158

 II.   Steps in Completing the PRINCE System 159

       Exercise 6.1:   Conducting a PRINCE Analysis 168

       Exercise 6.2:   Using Strategies 170

LISTING OF DISPLAYS

Figure 1.1: Basic Categories for Organizing Information on Public Policy Issues 3

Figure 1.2: Hypothetical Trend Projection Based on Trade between Great Britain and the American Colonies, 1769-1771 23

Figure 1.3: Positive Feedback Loop Diagram of the Relationship between Arbitrary Political Control and Population Growth in the American Colonies 26

Figure 1.4: Alternative Projections of Total Imports and Exports 33

Figure 4.1: Basic Graphic Format 102

Figure 4.2: Vertical Bar Graph 103

Figure 4.3: Bar Graph Variations 104

Figure 4.4: Trend Line 105

Figure 4.5: Pie Diagram 107

Figure 4.6: Scatterplots 121

Figure 4.7: Scatterplot of Test Scores and Grade Point Averages 122

Figure 4.8: Signs of X and Y in Four Quadrant Coordinate System 123

Figure 5.1: Potential Impact of Treatment on Time-Series Data 145

TABLE 1.1: Examples of Public Policy Issues 4

TABLE 1.2: Values in the Declaration of Independence 12

TABLE 1.3:   Summary of Guidelines for Monitoring Public
Policy Issues as Systematically and
Objectively as Possible 20

TABLE 1.4:   Contingency Table 25

TABLE 1.5:   Summary of Guidelines for Forecasting 27

TABLE 1.6:   Identification and Ranking of Values
in Declaration 29

TABLE 1.7:   Summary of Guidelines for Evaluating
Public Policy Issues 31

TABLE 1.8:   Summary of Guidelines for Prescribing
Public Policies 34

TABLE 4.1:   Motor Vehicle Travel in the U.S. 94

TABLE 4.2:   Gross National Product of Japan, 1950-
1970 in Five-Year Intervals 95

TABLE 4.3:   Gross National Product of Japan, 1950-
1970 in Five-Year Intervals 95

TABLE 4.4   Gross National Product of Japan and the
U.S., 1950-1970 in Five-Year Intervals 96

TABLE 4.5:   Properties of Measurement Scales 100

TABLE 4.6:   New York State Automobile Insurance
Premium Rates, 1950-1970 102

TABLE 4.7:   Age Distribution of Population Over
60 in 1974 106

TABLE 4.8:   Calculations for Standard Deviation 111

TABLE 4.9:   Contingency Table 115

TABLE 4.10:   Association of Sex and Party Affiliation 116

TABLE 4.11:   Association of Sex and Party Affiliation 117

TABLE 4.12:   Worksheet for Pearson's r -- Test Score/
GPA Data 125

TABLE 6.1:   PRINCE Chart 162

TABLE 6.2:   PRINCE Chart -- Maintain the Same Tuition
Cost from 1980-81 to 1981-82 166

<u>INTRODUCTION: A FRAMEWORK FOR STUDY</u>

<u>A public policy issue is a disagreement between two or more</u>
<u>elements of a society over the way that the society's government</u>
<u>deals with a given condition</u>. (The disagreement may be on how the
government is <u>actually</u> dealing with the condition, or how it <u>should</u>
deal with the condition.) There are three essential criteria derived
from this definition which determine whether or not a public policy
issue exists:

1. <u>Disagreement</u> between identifiable elements of the society.

2. <u>Societal conditions</u> affecting the society within which
    the disagreement exists.

3. <u>Governmental action</u> that will either occur or be seriously
    considered in order to deal with the condition.

Consider the following three situations. Each of them contains
one element of our definition, but none contains all of the three
required for classification as an issue.

1. Citizens of Columbus, Ohio accept a slight increase in
    their property taxes.

2. The mayor of Chicago, Illinois runs for re-election.

3. A sparse rainfall in parts of two Southern states creates
    hardship for many farmers.

Raising property taxes in Columbus, Ohio constitutes government
action dealing with a societal condition. But without any disagreement over the decision, it does not become a public issue. A mayor's
re-election campaign may involve disagreement among important elements of the city's voting public regarding the governmental actions

xi

that will follow as a consequence of the election results. However, the election itself does not represent a "societal condition." Finally, the low rainfall indicates a societal condition and some desire for action on the part of those farmers affected, but no widespread disagreement; in such a case the likelihood of governmental involvement is extremely low.

Of course, any of the three incidents could evolve into a public policy issue. To illustrate, we have changed the foregoing situations so that they satisfy the three criteria for being considered as public policy issues.

1. Many citizens of Columbus oppose the proposed
    increase in property taxes.

2. The mayor has declared that his re-election will
    signify support for a policy of extensive urban
    renewal in all decaying urban areas. His opponents
    oppose him primarily on this declaration.

3. Federal or State governmental aid is requested to
    assist the farmers affected by the drought.

The point is that only when all three characteristics occur simultaneously can we say a public issue exists.

Recognizing the circumstances constituting a particular public policy issue is only the first step in comprehending that issue. It doesn't tell us why the issue has developed; it doesn't tell us the factors instrumental in predicting the outcome of the issue. To achieve these things -- either as officials responsible for action or as effective observers and critics -- we need to organize a great deal of information on the issue, to understand the values underlying its development, and to analyze the information in the context of the values.

This learning package provides a framework through which these tasks can be completed. It is divided into six chapters. Chapter One deals with the basic concepts necessary to analyze public policy issues. Chapter Two and Chapter Three concern the acquisition of information necessary to the analysis. Chapter Two explores the use of many different data sources valuable in acquiring information. Chapter Three deals with another method of data collection -- surveys and interviews. Chapter Four explores the application of descriptive statistics in the analysis of public policy issues. Chapter Five concerns benefit-cost analysis of proposed public policies, a valuable skill in decision making and evaluation of public policies, and the use of scientific and quasi-scientific research designs in the analysis of public policy. Chapter Six, the PRINCE System, gives a method for predicting the outcome of the issue and strategies for changing the predicted outcome.

Chapters One through Four are based on the Policy Studies
Associates learning packages in the "Policy Sciences Series": PS-17,
Analyzing Public Policy Issues; PS-19, Library Research for the
Analysis of Public Policy; PS-12, Introduction to Surveys and Inter-
views; and PS-20, Descriptive Statistics for Public Policy Analysis.
Chapter Five is in part based on PS-11, Designs for Evaluating
Social Programs, and a forthcoming learning package on benefit-costs.
Chapter Six is adapted from Everyman's PRINCE: A Guide to Under-
standing Your Political Problems.

<u>CHAPTER ONE: ANALYZING PUBLIC POLICY ISSUES</u>

THE PRIMARY OBJECTIVE:

This chapter will introduce you to the basic concepts
necessary to analyze public policy.

UPON COMPLETION OF THIS CHAPTER, YOU WILL BE ABLE TO:

* Identify the elements of public policy issues within a
  framework that will enable you to formulate specific
  research tasks.

* Examine the role of public interest and special interest
  values in the analysis of public policy issues.

* Indicate the role of monitoring, forecasting, evaluation,
  and prescription in the analysis of public policy issues.

(Based on <u>PS-17: Analyzing Public Policy Issues</u>, William D. Coplin
and Michael K. O'Leary, Croton-on-Hudson, NY: Policy Studies
Associates, 1978.)

1

I: ORGANIZING INFORMATION ON PUBLIC POLICY ISSUES

Analyzing public policy issues involves dealing with two questions, which, though interconnected, are not the same. Public and private discussion of public policy frequently blurs these two questions, thereby confusing the discussion and analysis of public policy. Therefore, we want to begin our analysis by distinguishing between the two.

The first question is:

> What are the effects, both intended and unintended, of actual policies on various conditions in society?

The second question is:

> Why are certain policies established, while others are defeated, or not even considered at all?

The first question addresses the problem of evaluating the effects of public policy. Does a given decision have desirable or undesirable results -- or no results at all? Are all of these results anticipated, or, as it often happens, does policy produce some unexpected effects on society? The second question addresses the problems of the "politics of public policy." In other words, how do individuals and groups cooperate and compete in order to support and oppose alternative policies?

These two questions have a long endurance, stretching back in relevance to the American Revolution of 200 years ago. In the first place, a sufficient number of influential colonists had to decide they wanted to pursue the policy of independence, as opposed to other alternatives, such as trying to exert reformist pressure on their British overlords. For a long time, many Americans favored the latter course. The promulgation of the Declaration of Independence in 1776 by no means signified unanimous agreement that independence was the proper policy to follow.

Given a decision to declare independence, the second consideration was what effects would this have on the social, political, and economic lives of the Americans living in the former colonies?

And indeed, in the early war years, it was an open question whether the decision for independence would be able to take effect militarily, or if it would result in continued (or even increased) control by Great Britain -- just the opposite of what was intended.

A.   The Basic Framework: Environment, Actors, Policies

To organize information so that these two questions can be explored, we have found it helpful to use the classification scheme portrayed below:

Figure 1.1:   Basic Categories for Organizing
Information on Public Policy Issues

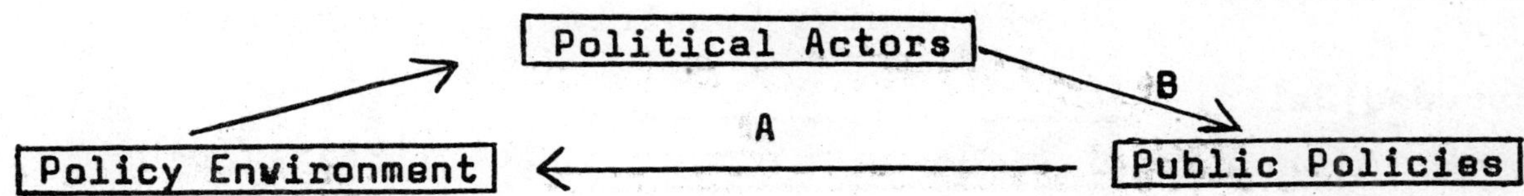

The figure suggests that it is necessary to obtain information on three specific components. First, we must consider the policy environment comprising these societal conditions that motivate political actors and serve as the targets of public policies. Secondly, we should be concerned with political actors, that is, individuals and groups that attempt to influence public policies. Finally, we are concerned with information regarding governmental laws and activities that collectively compose public policies. Table 1.1 provides examples of how one might apply the three categories to a variety of public policy issues.

Since the three terms -- policy environment, political actors, and public policies -- are synonomous with the three criteria developed from our definition, we know that if there is a public policy issue, it should be possible to obtain information on all three aspects. Moreover, the two arrows in the diagram, arrows "A" and "B", represent the two questions posed at the outset of this chapter. Once information has been gathered and organized to describe the policy environment, the political actors, and the

TABLE 1.1: Examples of Public Policy Issues

Policy Environment	Political Actors	Public Policies
Inflation	Consumers, Businessmen, Labor, Government Officials	Income Tax Levels
Traffic Congestion	Drivers, Taxpayers, Government Officials	* ___________
Poor Education in Urban Areas	Parents, Local School Officials, State School Officials	* ___________
* ___________	Oil Companies, Consumers, Oil-Producing Countries	Tariff on Oil Imports
Overcrowded Jails	* ___________ * ___________	Bail Bond Regulations, Parole Policies

*Where blanks appear, you are invited to supply your own examples.

public policies, it is then possible to explore the question of (1) the impact of the policies on the society (arrow "A") and (2) the pressures of political actors on the public policies (arrow "B"). The third portion of this chapter introduces procedures of analysis that can be employed for each of these questions. For the present, it is only necessary to make distinctions implicit in the diagram.

The classic document of the American revolution, the Declaration of Independence, clearly presents information classifiable into these three categories. The _actors_ include most prominently, of course, King George III of Great Britain. Other important actors mentioned are the Governors of the colonies who were subservient to the King, and his ministers in the homeland. The Declaration also directs a good deal of attention to the legislatures rendered impotent by the King, and colonial judges who interpret the law in what the signers felt was an unfair and tyrannical fashion. Finally, there is a guarded reference to the British citizenry and parliament: "...nor have We been wanting in attentions to our British brethren," continuing with, "We have warned them from time to time of attempts by their legislature..." Assertively, the Declaration took its message directly to the King.

The Declaration also provides a long list of <u>policies</u> which these actors have followed. These include: the King's refusal to "...Assent to Laws, the most wholesome and necessary for the public good..."; alternative dissolution or calling of secret legislature sessions "...for the sole purpose of fatiguing them into compliance with this measures..."; restriction of immigration into the colonies and prevention of people already in the colonies from becoming citizens; and the quartering of "...large bodies of armed troops among us...," whose interaction with the citizens suffered little judicial restraint.

The <u>environment</u> most prominent in the Declaration is, of course, the conditions in the colonies affected by these policies. The elements mentioned include, in the first instance, the repeated weaknesses of the Representative Houses, brought about by the policies of the King. Through this act, the King stifled the colonists' opposition to "...his invasions on the rights of the people." Other affected environmental conditions included the personal safety and security of the peoples in the colonies, which were frequently threatened by the King's armies; and, of course, the economic wealth of the colonists jeopardized by restrictions on foreign trade and by the imposition of "...taxes on us without our consent."

B.   <u>Summary</u>

To summarize, it is necessary to classify the information relevant to a public policy issue. The suggested classification requires that the following questions be answered:

a) What is the public policy?

b) What is the policy environment?

c) Who are the political actors?

d) What influence do the actors exert on the policy?

e) What impact does the policy have on the environment?

EXERCISE 1.1: Applying the Framework to a Public Policy Issue

Select three news articles from the <u>New York Times</u> which contain the criteria for public policy issues as outlined in this section. For each article, list the following items as they pertain to your article:

a) Environment

b) Actors

c) Policy

d) Arrow "A"

e) Arrow "B"

II: ORGANIZING VALUES ON PUBLIC POLICY ISSUES

The driving force behind all public policy issues is the
conflict between individuals and groups over conditions existing
in the society and possible governmental remedies. Conflict
arises due to the differing values held by groups or individuals.
Consequently, most information on public policy issues is imbued
with the values of those responsible for the gathering and presentation of the information.

For that reason, it is very important in organizing the
value dimension of public policy issues to separate facts from
meaning of, and relationship between, values and facts. However,
for our purposes, a _factual_ statement can be defined as one
describing or predicting conditions or events, and a _value_ statement as one rendering a positive or negative judgement about a
particular condition or event.

At the outset, one guide to making the distinction between
facts and values is through examining the verbs used in a given
statement. If a statement contains verbs like "is" or "are"
or "will be," it is a factual statement. If the statement contains
verbs like "should" or "ought to," it is value statement. Unfortunately, those people likely to make statements on public policy
issues are frequently unclear about the distinction between values
and facts. The rhetoric underlying most public policy issue
discussion and analysis frequently fails to make this critical
distinction.

The Declaration contains many statements asserted as fact, but
which are actually value claims of the leaders of the American
Revolution. The statement "[that] to secure these rights, governments are instituted among men," reflects a value judgement, not
an expression of fact. Governments are instituted for many different reasons, not all of them nearly as noble as those claimed in
the Declaration. This is a common tactic in policy rhetoric.
Therefore, you must look beyond grammatical construction to analyze
a statement. One good rule of thumb is: Can the statement be
tested with some available evidence? If it can, it is a factual
statement (even though it may turn out to be untrue in the light of
such evidence). If, on the other hand, it cannot be tested with

evidence, as the statements quoted above from the Declaration, then it is a value statement.

However difficult to carry out, the distinction between facts and values should be maintained if the analysis of public policy issues is to be a useful enterprise. This will become apparent when we discuss the types of policy analysis.

For the remainder of this section, we will introduce value considerations typically underlying public policy issues. Basically, two types can be identified -- those classified as self-interest, and those classified as part of a larger concern for the society as a whole. Both types pervade most public policy issues.

A.   Self-interest Values

To the degree that basic societal needs are not satisfied, and the perception persists that governmental action can make a difference, those individuals and groups affected will attempt to obtain policy decisions protective of goods and services desired by them. Central city merchants lobbying for improvements in a local urban transportation system exemplify such an effort.

It is generally the case that the needs of individuals and groups are satisfied. Governmental institutions attempt to build support by serving the needs of their citizens. They are in the business of satisfying needs and usually do so. When these needs are satisfied, public policy issues do not arise. However, there are occasions when the needs of groups and individuals are not satisfied, occurring under conditions in which the government itself is unaware and usually of a temporary nature. Continued dissatisfaction will almost certainly result in government becoming aware of the needs of other groups and individuals may emerge who are opposed for one reason or another. When opposition arises between groups, public issues arise.

Opposition can be direct or indirect. _Direct opposition_ is characterized by two groups or individuals holding contrapositive positions on the same issue, e.g., group A opposes the demand for certain services that group B requests. _Indirect opposition_ occurs when the demands by one group can only be satisfied at the expense of the satisfaction of demands of another group.

While the Declaration clearly emphasized general public interest or societal values, it is not without reference to specific values emanating from the self-interest of the colonies. For example, the emphasis on economic questions relating to taxation and trade regulation was motivated primarily by the feeling by certain members of the colonies that Great Britain was receiving a disproportionate share of goods generated by the colonies. There was a claim that the taxes were unjust because they were imposed without the consent of the colonies. However, the increased cost to the colonies represented by rising taxes was the major complaint. As we shall see, the transformation of statements originating from self-interest into statements based on public interest values is more than a rhetorical trick.

B. Public Interest Values

Frequently, public policy issues commence as conflicts between a few groups over their particular self-interests. However, if the issue remains unresolved and the opposing groups grow more adamant and stronger in numbers and power, broader values are frequently cited. It is not always clear whether these broader values are raised in order to enlist the support of others not directly affected by self-interest, or whether, in fact, the groups involved actually feel such values are at stake. At some point, however, such societal concerns do become important in almost all major public policy issues.

It is possible to identify six major public interest values that emerge in one form or another in public policy issues:

    a) Individual freedom,

    b) Order within the society,

    c) Equality among individuals,

    d) Justice for individuals,

    e) Legitimate decision-making process, and

    f) Efficiency of government operations.

A variety of definitions and interpretations of a public interest value can be cited as one reason for the conflict these values generate. Individual freedom obviously does not mean that individuals can do anything they want. They cannot break the law to satiate individual desire. Each society has spent vast sums of intellectual effort in an attempt to delimit the concept of freedom, but it is clear that definitions and applications are continually changing.

The same can be said for the remaining five values: order, equality, justice, legitimate decision-making process, and governmental efficiency. These terms appear throughout the history of all societies, continually requiring refinement of definition and application. <u>Order</u> connotes the maintenance of existing community laws and relationships, but no community can exist without changing those laws and relationships. <u>Equality</u> is grounded in the concept that each member of the community is equal to another member of the community, but no society has such a condition (although some are closer to it than others). <u>Justice</u> refers to the fair treatment of individuals by the government, others in the society, or before the law, but 'fairness' is a fluid concept and applied erratically. <u>Efficiency</u> can be estimated in terms of resources required to accomplish a given objective, but the 'soft' nature of most objectives make it easy for reasonable people to disagree over the expected efficiency of a given governmental policy. Finally, everyone agrees that <u>governmental decisions should be reached in compliance with those legal and moral principles</u> usually associated with the democratic process. However, few agree on the exact content of those principles and their application in specific situations.

Because it is impossible to formally define and apply these five values across all conditions within any given society and with respect to any given public policy issues, actors frequently interpret the values to support their particular position. On any given public policy issue, two opposing groups may find that the same value leads them to opposing views on the issue. For example, the freedom of the British and French aviation industry to land a supersonic jet in the United States during 1976 was perceived by many individuals and groups as an infringement on their freedom from excessive noise. Everyone to some extent values freedom, order, equality, justice, government efficiency, and legitimate procedures as we have defined them, but their definitions and applications to concrete public policy issues create the disagreement that is an inherent part of that issue.

Not only does disagreement among groups or individuals arise because of different interpretations of the same value; it also arises because one value conflicts with another. If all individuals were free to do what they wanted -- including not paying taxes -- there would be no order; individuals would not be equal; there would be no basis for the fair treatment of everyone; and governmental operations and decision making would grind to a halt. Similarly, order may require a curtailment of individual freedom, the maintenance of the status quo, and in some extreme cases, the elimination of fair treatment to specific individuals and groups within a society, or the wasteful application of resources. Equal treatment also may require the curtailment of individual freedoms, the reduction of stability, the abandonment of just procedures, or

the adoption of inefficient methods. Justice for one individual
may limit the freedom of the other, the maintenance of order, the
reduction of equality of opportunity, or the slowing down of
governmental processes. Policies that are efficient from the point
of view of achieving specific objectives may reduce freedoms,
threaten order, or be inherently unequal or unjust. Finally,
the pursuit of legitimate decision-making procedures would not
limit the opposition to policies threatening the other five values.

It is not surprising, therefore, to be confronted by public
policy issues where one group defends its position by citing one
of these six values, while another group occupies an opposing
position by citing another value. For example, some groups involved
in the elimination of segregation in the public schools operate
on the principle of equality among individuals. Those opposing
it do so on grounds of maintaining order, the efficient operation
of schools, or the protection of individual freedom. Clearly,
these major societal values do not provide clear guidelines that
can be easily applied to resolve public policy issues.

Rather, they as frequently help to increase the intensity of
disagreement among groups involved in those issues as they do to
reach an acceptable position.

The existence of and tension among these six values are evident
in the Declaration. Table 1.2 lists passages representing each
of the six public interest values discussed.

All six values appear to provide general support for the
position of the Declaration; yet it is possible to envision some
conflict among them. In fact, the strong symbolic emphasis on
equality at the beginning of the Declaration was not reinforced
by specific grievances in the remainder of the document. We know
from the record of the debate over the wording of the Declaration
that the Southern colonies blocked an attempt by the Jeffersonian
camp to refer to slavery as an evil. Similarly, it was possible
to excuse some of the actions of King George on the grounds of
the efficiency of governmental operations. Although these
potential value conflicts are relatively obscure in the Declaration,
they almost always arise in discussions of public policy issues.

TABLE 1.2:   Values in the Declaration of Independence

VALUES	QUOTATION FROM DECLARATION
1. Freedom of the individual	"Life, Liberty and the pursuit of happiness."
2. Order within society	"He has excited domestic insurrections amongst us..."
3. Equality among individuals	"All men are created equal."
4. Justice for individuals	"For depriving us in many cases, of the benefits of Trial by Jury."
5. Legitimacy of decision-making process	"He has forbidden his Governors to pass Laws of immediate and pressing importance, unless suspended in their operation till his Assent should be obtained; and when so suspended, he has utterly neglected to attend to them."
6. Efficiency of government operations	"He has called together legislative bodies at places unusual, uncomfortable, and distant from the depository of public Records."

OPTIONAL EXERCISE: The Good Society Exercise

(We suggest you defer reading this section until after completing the game which appears in the Appendix.)

"The Good Society Exercise," is designed to demonstrate the role of these six values in the governance of societies. Although the exercise is a highly abstracted version of actual political processes, repeated experimental runs of the game have demonstrated the trade-offs among the six values. The Society consists of groups with different levels of power as well as a powerful Central Authority (i.e., government). The poor groups usually agitate for

more power, while the rich groups try to enlist the support of
Central Authority in protecting their power. Central Authority
is frequently faced with a choice between supporting equality (and
therefore the demands of the poor groups for more power) and
supporting order (and therefore the demands of the rich). Questions
concerning the legitimacy of the decision-making process and the
efficiency of governmental operations, as well as justice and freedom, are raised when petitions are formed to change the structure
of the Good Society.

Several general patterns have emerged from repeated use of
this game in a variety of educational settings that correspond to
the dynamics of the American Revolution. In the first place, the
members of Central Authority almost inevitably define the "Good
Society" as one in which their power is either maintained or
increased. The other groups usually begin the exercise with an
ambivalent attitude toward the Central Authority. On the one hand,
the groups fear Central Authority because it has so much power;
but, on the other hand, at least some of the groups look to
Central Authority for help in redressing the grievances they have
in the so-called Good Society .

In those cases where Central Authority has been receptive to
requests for help from the groups and attempted to appear to be
concerned with their interests, Central Authority has survived
throughout the exercise with its power relatively intact. Conversely, in those cases when the members of Central Authority
decide that its power is so great that it need not appear to be
responsive to the other groups, the groups usually find a way to
unite and strip Central Authority of its powers.

The results of the exercise have obvious analogies with situations confronting governments. National governments must be
responsive to those groups upon whose acceptance their authority
depends. Otherwise, these nominally authoritative actors will
have less capacity to determine national policies.

It should thus be clear that however important authoritative
actors are in understanding policymaking, it is equally important
to study those groups upon whose support the authority for policy
depends.

C.   <u>Values in the Analysis of Public Policy Issues</u>

We have discussed the need to distinguish between values and
facts and described the role of values attributable to self-
interest and public interest concerns. Unless one clearly comes
to grips with the values inherent in a public policy issue, the

resulting analysis will not be very valuable. Not only must the analyst understand the value basis invoked by the various actors with respect to a specific public policy issue, but he must also understand how his own values relate to that issue. Because our concern centers on analysis seeking the decision-making process, we need to emphasize that an important part of that analysis is the extent to which the analysts recognize their own value biases.

We therefore suggest that when studying a public policy issue you attempt to identify the values operating on the major actors in the issue, and the values which you hold.

EXERCISE 1.2: Value Analysis

A value conflict occurs when individuals or groups assign different priorities and assessments to conditions which affect them as a result of differences in values. Using one or more public interest values, write a paragraph on a value conflict present in a public policy issue.

III: TYPES OF PUBLIC POLICY ANALYSIS -- MONITORING, FORECASTING, EVALUATION, AND PRESCRIPTION

This section introduces the basic elements of four kinds of public policy analysis:

Monitoring (Descriptive), that is, recording system-atically patterns of events and conditions over time;

Forecasting (Predictive), that is, projecting what patterns might emerge in the future;

Evaluating (Evaluative), that is, assessing the degree to which conditions and events have become better or worse according to a given set of standards;

Prescribing (Prescriptive), that is, suggesting and assessing alternative courses of actions that are designed to improve conditions according to a given set of standards.

These four activities can be illustrated by looking at how investors might view the Dow Jones industrial average within each of the four tasks in order to make decisions on how to increase their returns. Investors compute this average by analyzing the 30 most important industrial stocks. The "average" is merely the sum of the increases and/or decreases in the stocks divided by 30. This measure is used as one indicator of the industrial health of the nation. If the Dow Jones industrial average is continually rising, then industry in the United States is growing profitably with a steady return on investments. If the average shows a steady decline, then we suspect that the business and investment climate in the nation is not very good. The average is most useful to analysts when they observe its movements over time, as for example, a 30-day period.

The Dow Jones industrial average can serve as a tool for analyzing the policy choices which confront an investor. First, the average can be used to monitor the daily fluctuations in prices. Secondly, it can be used as a basis for forecasting whether a set of stocks, or even one stock, will rise or fall.

Thirdly, the average can be used as a standard against which the performance of a particular stock can be evaluated -- the degree it has performed for better or worse than those represented in the average. Finally, by looking at the performance of a set of stocks in relation to the average and using a forecast of the future performance of the average, it is possible to decide which stock would be the most profitable investment opportunity.

We are not saying that the Dow Jones average is a perfect tool for monitoring, forecasting, evaluating, or prescribing investment decisions. Anyone who has invested in the stock market knows there are no perfect tools. However, it does serve as a general procedure for organizing information to perform the kinds of analyses that allow one to make decisions. Although there are no guarantees, it is generally true that with respect to any decision the systematic performance of these four types of analysis is better than performing no analysis.

In this section, we will discuss each of the four types of analysis, continuing to draw our illustrations from the Declaration of Independence. We will also discuss the data collection and analysis techniques associated with each of the four types of analysis.

A.   <u>Monitoring</u>

The most essential and basic of the four analytical tasks is monitoring. No intelligent discussion of any public policy issue can occur unless you are aware of the past and present record of the policy environment, political actors, and public policies. Although there is agreement on the importance of such information, there is less agreement on what that information is, and how to obtain and present it. This section provides some guidelines on collecting and using information to monitor public policy issues.

We have already discussed previously how the authors of the Declaration of Independence described the policy environment, political actors, and public policies relevant to the issue of the American colonies' decision to declare independence from England. All of the information cited represents monitoring of the issue. The Declaration's authors introduced monitoring information with the sentence "To prove this, let Facts be submitted to a candid world." In phrasing their introduction this way, they specified that their monitoring or recounting of history was performed in order to support their position on the issue of independence.

Today, however, many scholars assert that the use of history to prove one's public policy position is a limited one. In fact, some scholars would say that it is a misuse of monitoring --

monitoring should present an objective picture of reality. The
'objective' ideal conflicts with the very nature of information
collection and communication. Kenneth Boulding has best presented
this view in a book entitled The Image, arguing that an image is
'internalized' or subjective knowledge of one's environment, past
experiences, future expectations, and values.[1] Imagery consists
of a set of attitudes, value judgments, and behavioral assumptions.
It is also composed of symbols which subjectively represent reality,
at the same time prescribing, predicting, and commanding action.
The image is a result of people's perceptive and evaluative capa-
bilities and aids individuals to operate in their millieu. The
most generic of all psychological mechanisms, it provides for the
individual a basis for action because it locates each individual in
time and space, in a field of personal relations, in a world of
dynamic operations, and in the midst of "subtle intimations and
emotions." As a process, the image acts upon and, in turn, is
acted upon by the individual. The social development of the individual and the evolution of each person's view of society are not
two distinct processes but aspects of the same process.

While recognizing the validity of Boulding's description of
information acquisition and collection, we also need to recognize
the need for people to maintain what Boulding calls 'open images',
that is, frameworks which can absorb and adapt to new information.
This is particularly important in the dialogue over public policy
issues. It is likely that different actors have images producing
conflicting information, which, in turn, render impossible the
compromise and consensus necessary for the effective operation of
public policy. In addition, because public policy issues involve
intense conflict between various groups, third parties having an
indirect interest are likely to play a large role in the final
decision. For example, the leaders of European nations played an
influential role in the American War of Independence and therefore
were central targets of the authors of the Declaration of Independence. To the extent that the record is accumulated and presented in such a way that such third parties consider it to be
"fair" and "accurate," the monitoring is more likely to generate
support. Furthermore, some individuals for one reason or another
take no position and therefore attempt to monitor conditions as
fairly and accurately as possible. Therefore, whether one has a
position on an issue or is merely seeking to present information
that will help you develop a position, steps need to be taken in
monitoring which make the collection and presentation of the
information as systematic and objective as possible.

---

[1] Kenneth E. Boulding, The Image: Knowledge in Life and Society,
Ann Arbor: University of Michigan Press, 1961, p. 5.

But how does one collect and present information on public policy issues as systematically and objectively as possible? This question, a continuing concern of social scientists, cannot be answered easily or simply. Over the years, a variety of procedures have been developed to increase both the systematic and the objective basis of information. To introduce these procedures and their application to the analysis of public policy issues, we first need to have a definition of systematic and objective.

<u>Systematic</u> refers to the degree to which all relevant information is collected and presented. Unfortunately, it is not possible to do this completely. Even if we restricted the scope to information on just the policy environment, as opposed to all three components -- the policy environment, political actors, and public policies -- there is no way that any individual or team of individuals can collect and represent information that would totally monitor a public policy issue. Fortunately, there are methods of creating samples of information that are a valid representation of the whole. The most obvious example of this is the administration of an opinion poll to a representative segment of an entire population. Other methods of examining a representative sample include the application of quantitative analysis to written information, and the direct observation of conditions.

By <u>objective</u>, we mean that the information represents the reality it is supposed to reflect. As previously noted, the role of images and the interpretative nature of the language of public policy issue discussion make it very difficult to keep researcher bias out of the information collection and presentation process.

Techniques guarding against bias include documentation, presentation of comparative information, the detailing of facts, the procedures of collecting information, and the use of multiple sources of information. Each of these techniques allows the audience to render its own judgement.

These guidelines cannot always be followed. Frequently, a long discourse on documentary sources or the representative quality of a particular sample will bore or confuse an audience, even if that audience consists of people vitally concerned with the issue. Moreover, the costs associated with complying fully with financial or deadline restrictions, or both, may make it impossible to follow these guidelines. Furthermore, to fully comply with them might require the use of quantitative data and sophisticated data analysis techniques beyond the grasp of those directly responsible for the decision. Finally, it is possible that even those techniques available will not work because the information is not available in a form allowing for collection and presentation.

To illustrate, we turn again to the Declaration of Independence which contains a long list of grievances, representing an attempt to monitor the policy environment. Not surprisingly, the list does not follow the systematic format outlined above. As stated, these guidelines cannot always be followed. Time factors as well as lack of knowledge of sophisticated data techniques in the colonial period prohibited the authors of the Declaration from monitoring the policy environment, using methods available to today's policymakers. If the authors were fortunate enough to have had the time and knowledge of today's policymakers, the Declaration could have been more effectively constructed. A listing of a cross-section of acts taken by England as well as a list of what the colonies did to provoke some of these actions would have pre-sented a clearer and fuller picture of that period.

If the authors had been familiar with methods of data collec-tion, better documentation and more specificity could have been included in the document. The Declaration employs phrases such as "quartering of troops" and "swarms of officials." This infor-mation would have been more meaningful to the readers, and possibly more persuasive, if numerical information could have been incorporated.

Nevertheless, the Declaration remains an instructive example for reviewing the framework of public policy analysis. It is also an excellent reference to show how these methods have developed over the years into sophisticated, systematic, and objective approaches to analysis. If our forefathers were aware of these sophisticated approaches, it is very likely that the Declaration would have included graphs of trade patterns and tax rates, dates and specifics on the suspension of legislatures, and a survey of Americans to determine the degree to which they felt harassed. Admittedly, such additions may not compare favorably with the stirring rhetoric of the Declaration. However, given the complexity of modern life, the nature of contemporary public policy issues, and the plethora of publicity, the monitoring of information today needs to be consistent with the guidelines described in this section.

Table 1.3 below summarizes the discussion on these guide-lines.

B.   Forecasting

All discussions of public policy issues concern themselves with the future, since expectations about conditions in the policy environment stimulate political actors to debate alternative public policies. As will be seen, forecasting methods run the gamut from the unstated implications of monitoring statements to

TABLE 1.3: Summary of Guidelines for Monitoring Public Policy
Issues as Systematically and Objectively as Possible

SELECTION OF INFORMATION COLLECTED AND PRESENTED	EVIDENCE OF ACCURACY OF INFORMATION
1. Provide a basis for comparison over time or across similar conditions.	Provide documentation of information.
2. Draw a sample of information that represents the subject in an unbiased way.	Use multiple sources of information.
3. Use surveys where applicable.	Provide detailed information.
4. Use as much quantitative information as possible.	Describe methods of collecting information.

---

elaborate computer models. Again, the forecasting may be done
with respect to all three categories in the basic public policy
framework (actors, policies, environment), although the primary
focus of attention, as in the case of monitoring, is on the
evolution of conditions in the policy environment.

This is typical of most of the forecasting that appears in
the informal analysis of public policy issues. The Declaration,
for example, states that "the history of the present King of
Great Britain is a history of repeated injuries and usurpations,"
and then makes the key prediction of the document: "all having in
direct objective the establishment of an absolute Tyranny over
these states." The forecast is typical because it uses two common
bases for such predictions. The first is simple extrapolation from
the past into the future. The authors present the record of events
and conditions of the past as evidence of the existence of an
absolute tyranny. It is assumed that matters will continue to
deteriorate. The second is the attribution of motivation to the
King. It is argued that the evidence indicates that the King
"evinces a design to reduce them under absolute Despotism" which
can be used to forecast his future tyrannical behavior.

The use of trend projection is a widely used but crude basis for forecasting. Trend projection is based on the assumption that what has been happening will continue to happen, frequently with increased speed. It is crude because it fails to recognize "break points" or critical thresholds which might result in changes of a trend, although it is frequently the only basis for making a forecast -- particularly when the conditions are unique -- as in the case of the Revolution.

Motivational analysis is used in public policy issue research when there are a few key actors whose values and images appear to be able to shape conditions. It is more frequently employed in the prediction of the behavior of political actors and the evolution of public policies than in the forecast of conditions in the political environment. Its main limitation is that it is virtually impossible to be sure of the motivations of most human beings, particularly those in powerful political positions. Usually, multiple goals and a variety of other actors influence the key political actors, meaning that the basis for such actors' behavior could alter radically.

We are not saying, however, that trend projections or motivational analysis should be avoided in forecasting public policy issues. Our point is that such approaches to forecasting are based on a variety of untestable assumptions. To the degree that you have access to the information necessary for testing such assumptions, the confidence in the forecast increases. We will now briefly examine forms of forecasting that make the assumptions underlying the forecasts more explicit and testable than the kinds of informal and implicit predictions appearing in the Declaration.

1. Explicit Verbal Forecasts

By listing grievances, the Declaration attempts to establish the basis for its forecast. If the monitoring statements could have conformed more closely to the contemporary techniques outlined previously, the verbal forecasts themselves could have carried more weight. In addition, if the colonists had access to the appropriate data, they could have indeed more effectively criticized the King's actions. Their arguments could have been more convincing if they presented an analysis of influences on the King as well as the past record of the King in other situations.

The key to improving verbal forecasts is the clear statement, in propositional terms, of the assumptions underlying the forecast. A proposition is a statement of the relationship between two or more variables that can be examined further. The propositional format for the major prediction in the Declaration might have been "within a given society, the occurrence of despotic behavior at one time period leads to an increase of such behavior in subsequent time periods." Stated in this way, it is clear that both assumptions are open to serious questioning. Even so, it would improve the forecasting basis of the document as it would allow readers to relate similar circumstances to test the proposition on their own.

An additional method of making explicit the basis of verbal forecasts is the use of a _scenario_. A scenario is a statement of the likely evolution of a set of interrelated events and conditions. The authors of the Declaration could have used a scenario to delineate how they thought present conditions would lead to an absolute dictatorship. The value of such a method is that it clarifies the assumptions underlying a forecast and allows the audience to examine in specific detail the logical relationship between events and conditions. An additional value of the scenario is that it forces the analyst to imagine alternative courses of events, sometimes introducing new assumptions that might have been ignored.

An even more powerful method of introducing new assumptions is the use of _role-playing or gaming techniques_. The Good Society Exercise, presented in the Appendix, exemplifies a role-playing exercise which explores methods of establishing decision-making structures. Such structures are designed to achieve particular values. Exercises similar to the Good Society Exercise, but placing greater emphasis on specific public policy content, can be used to identify assumptions underlying public policy forecasts. Although the construction of the exercise and the participation by a number of individuals entails a substantial investment of time and effort, it can help to generate a wide variety of forecasts that can be examined through other techniques.

Scenarios and role-playing exercises can help to increase the variety of forecasts as well as the range of assumptions underlying such forecasts. They can be used to supplement interpretations obtained by monitoring the conditions surrounding a public policy issue. Although they do not necessarily lead to improving the explicit nature of verbal forecasts, the tasks of scenario writing or role playing can generate the basis for more systematically exploring assumptions.

2. Formalizing Forecasts

The necessity for stating forecasts in propositional terms has already been discussed. There are three reasons for this need. First, propositional analysis increases the awareness of both the writer and the audience of the intellectual basis for the forecast. Secondly, using the method makes it easier to test the forecast with information from relevant examples. Finally, it provides a basis for assessing the validity of the forecast as events and conditions unfold. For these reasons, it is important to state forecasts in propositional terms.

Once so stated, it is easier to generate and evaluate predictions using a number of new techniques. We will briefly discuss two classes of such techniques -- statistical methods and computer simulation.

a)   Statistical Techniques

Of all the formal forecasting methods, statistical techniques are the most widely used. Although we cannot provide an exhaustive discussion of such techniques here, we can illustrate their use in generating and evaluating forecasts. Statistical techniques, including the use of graphs and charts, are methods for organizing quantitative data for the purpose of exploring propositional statements.

The time-series graph, similar to the one pictured below, is a well-accepted representation of trend projection. Figure 1.2 applies a time-series graph to information posited in the Declaration.

Figure 1.2:   Hypothetical Trend Projection Based on Trade between Great Britain and the American Colonies, 1769-1771.

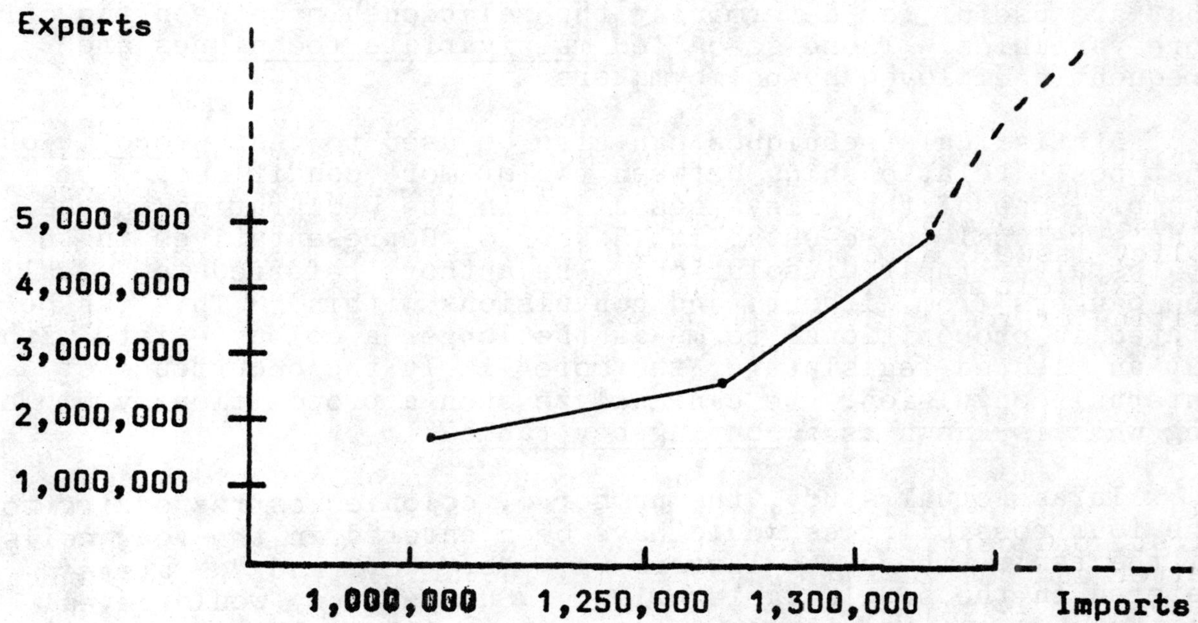

Source: Oliver M. Dickerson, The Navigation Acts and the American Revolution, Philadelphia: University of Pennsylvania, 1951.

The graph portrays the relationship between the colonies' imports to England and England's exports to America. By extending the graph into the future (represented by the dotted lines), the forecast is made more explicit. The writers of the Declaration could have used such a graph to strengthen their arguments regarding dominance by England. As the colonies attempted to become self-sufficient by making their own products, and so forth, England forced the colonies to purchase her goods. And when the colonies' imports to Britain slightly increased, these forced exports on the colonies increased tremendously.

One can also derive a statistical measure stating this relationship between imports and exports. This measure is called Pearson's product-moment correlation (usually symbolized with the letter "r") and is expressed with a number ranging from -1.0 to +1.0. To the extent that r approaches +1.0, the export and import rate will rise at the same time. To the extent that it approaches -1.0, the forced exports are decreasing while imports increase. The particular correlation for Figure 1.2 is +0.94, indicating, as the Declaration suggested, that exports were tied to imports.

Many statistical techniques can be utilized in public policy analysis. Forecasts can be interpreted through analysis of various visual display techniques and through statistical measures. Central tendencies of information can be summarized by employing means and medians. <u>Bar Graphs</u> are useful for comparing conditions in different areas. There also exists many measures of association that are useful for determining the relationship between two or more variables. These so-called <u>multivariate techniques</u> are frequently employed by policymakers.

Statistical techniques can also be used to test <u>propositions</u> that posit relationships between two or more conditions. For example, one of the grievances cited in the Declaration is the King's refusal to re-establish Houses of Representatives in the states after their dissolution. The authors referred to "...all the dangers from without, and convulsions within." This can be stated in propositional terms as the longer a colony exists without an elected legislature, the more likely the occurrence of internal convulsion. We can analyze such a proposition by employing what is known as a <u>contingency table</u>.

In an actual study, the number of colonies corresponding to the four possibilities would have been entered in the four cells of the table (where the letters "a," "b," "c," and "d" are entered in the sample table below). Such a study would reveal that most colonies without a legislature had a large amount of internal convulsion. Therefore, box "c" would have a relatively large number. After entering numbers in all the cells of the contingency table, it is possible to calculate a measure of association for the joint occurrences. This is done by employing

TABLE 1.4: Contingency Table

Number of Colonies With:

		High Amounts of Convulsion	Low Amounts of Convulsion
Number of Colonies:	with a legislature	a	b
	without a legislature	c	d

a statistic known as Yule's Q. The statistic Q, like the correlation statistic "r," discussed above, can range from -1.0 to +1.0. A value of -1.0 means perfect negative correlation, +1.0 means perfect positive correlation, and 0.0 means no correlation.

b) Computer Simulation Model

In recent years, a special technique for handling predictions involving a number of variables with complex relationships has emerged. Known as computer simulation model, this technique employs use of a systematized set of relationships to calculate the relationships among factors in order to generate a forecast. While the mastery of the total technique requires substantial expertise, it is possible to show the basic characteristics of the approach in a few pages.

The most critical first step in devising a simulation model is to produce a pictorial representation of the relationship among the factors, or, as we shall call them, variables. Such a pictorial representation is frequently referred to as a causal loop diagram.

The Declaration of Independence contained many forecasts of how the social and economic environment in the New World would evolve if present trends and conditions continued. Many of these environmental conditions had a mutual feedback effect on one another. That is, the more that one condition increased (or decreased) the more that another condition increased (or decreased) because of their mutual effects on each other. An example of this is the relationship mentioned in the Declaration between two conditions:

(1) Arbitrary political control exercised by the King over
     the colonies, and

(2) Restriction of population growth in the colonies.

On one hand, the writers explicitly asserted that the more
arbitrary political control was exercised, the more there was
restriction on population growth. On the other hand, what they
implied was that the more population growth was restricted, the
more arbitrary political control could be easily exercised over the
smaller population. This is what social scientists call a <u>positive
feedback loop</u> and is symbolized in the following figure:

Figure 1.3: Positive Feedback Loop Diagram of the
             Relationship between Arbitrary Political
             Control and Population Growth in the
             American Colonies

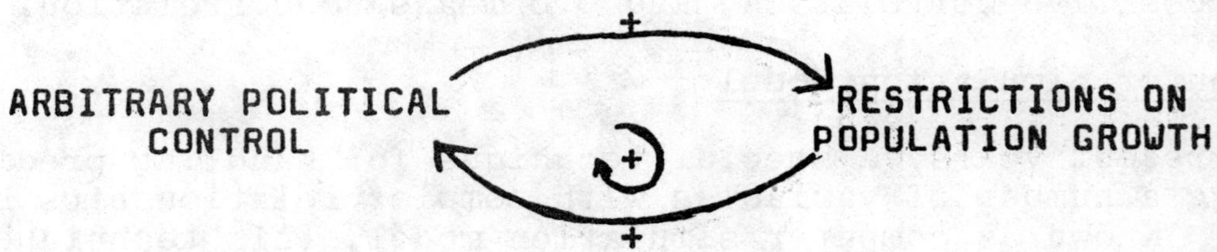

(The + in the middle of the two factors either increase
       or decrease at the same time.)

The forecast produced by this line of reasoning -- whether
presented verbally as in the Declaration, or symbolically, as
above -- is that both authoritarian political control and population growth restrictions would continue to grow indefinitely
into the future unless something interfered to change the relationship. It was just such an "interference" that was represented by
the call for independence and revolution issued by the American
leaders. The same forecast was made here through both verbal and
symbolic presentations of a simple aspect of the social environment
in the colonies. There is, however, a special advantage in using
the symbolic form when dealing with many different elements in a
complex environment. In recent years, social scientists have
developed techniques to enter such models of relationships into a
computer to simulate the dynamics of even very complex environments,
thereby producing forecasts for policy analysis.

In the foregoing, we have surveyed a variety of techniques and guidelines relevant to the forecasting of conditions and events associated with public policy issues. The available techniques range from very informal statements to statistical analysis and computer-based simulation. However, as in the case of monitoring, it is not always possible to use more systematic techniques given the nature of the audience or the amount of time and money available. At the very least, however, the intellectual basis for forecasts should be articulated as clearly as possible.

Table 1.5 below summarizes the points in this section.

TABLE 1.5:   Summary of Guidelines for Forecasting

---

1. Clearly identify what you are forecasting and the time frame.

2. Present factual information in making forecast.

3. State the underlying assumptions used to get from the present to the future.

4. Use quantitative data, statistical analysis, graphic displays, role playing, and computer simulation to explore different underlying assumptions.

C. Evaluation

Just as concern for the future underscores the growth of public policy issues, disagreement over the worth of existing public policies plays a major role in the growth and outcome of public policy issues. As a result of this, the analysis of public policy issues must measure existing and future conditions against the values of those most affected by the policies. The value types affected by public policy issues, and demonstrating how the Declaration of Independence augmented both self-interest and public interest values in the analysis of the independence issues, were discussed earlier in this chapter.

This section will describe procedures for the systematic application of values to public policy issues. The informal method of application exercised in the Declaration was a listing of grievances in the form of specific criticisms of King George's actions. The evidence presented clearly demonstrated that

self-interest values, such as economic benefit and the public
interest values of order and legitimate governmental decision
making, were threatened. However, the inference as to which
values were threatened was left up to the reader, and the failure
to apply other values such as equality, lacked the systematic
approach that is important in the evaluation of contemporary
public policy issues.

Two basic steps are required to systematically evaluate a
public policy issue. The first step is to determine which values
are to be used in the evaluation. The second step is to collect
information useful in determing the degree to which those values
are realized. Generally, policy evaluation is focused on the
degree to which a given public policy contributes to conditions
conforming to specific values in the policy environment. Occasionally, evaluations focus on the legitimacy of the decision-
making processes, leading to a specific public policy and its
implementation. In the following, we will discuss the two basic
steps with respect to both questions.

1.   Identifying Values

How a variety of values surround most public policy issues,
and how ambiguously stated such values are, has been previously
discussed. The multiple and ambiguous nature of this value
dimension makes it difficult and sometimes impossible to conduct
systematic evaluation. However, this is a reality of public
policy issue analysis that must be recognized and dealt with as
effectively as possible. The first and most critical step is to
identify each of the values involved, and, if possible, to list
them in order of importance.

We have already cited both self-interest and public interest
values that underlie the Declaration of Independence, and noted
how ambiguity and conflict could have been avoided. However, it
is possible to clarify an order for the values. Table 1.6 lists
the values in order of importance, why we think they follow that
order, and a specific definition of the terms. No doubt,
historians of that period might find themselves disagreeing with
these interpretations. It is possible, however, to formalize
the value dimensions by examining the degree to which the document
makes specific references to the values concerned. The table provides, as evidence for the priorities, a rough count of the themes
in the 27 grievances listed in the Declaration.

Table 1.6 establishes both priorities and a clear definition
of the values applied to the issue of independence. In reading
through the table, it should be obvious that both the definitions
and the priority estimates would not produce unanimous agreement
among the signers of the Declaration. The lack of agreement is

TABLE 1.6: Identification and Ranking of Values in Declaration

VALUES	DEFINITION	EVIDENCE FOR PRIORITIES
1. Legitimacy of decision making.	Customary and legal procedures for making and administering laws.	37% (10 of 27) of the grievances refer to failure to allow normal decision—making processes to operate.
2. Order within society.	Action to minimize chances of violence from both within and without.	33% (9 of 27) of the grievances refer to violent acts or promoting conditions for violence.
3. Economic interests.	Action to increase opportunities for economic growth or decrease economic loss.	15% (4 of 27) of the grievances list actions affecting economic conditions.
4. Justice for individuals.	The maintenance of rules for fair treatment of individuals by the government.	15% (4 of 27) of the grievances clearly identify infringements on the operation of the law with respect to the individual. Several other grievances indirectly mention this concern.
5. Freedom for individuals.	The maintenance of rules and conditions so that individuals can exercise basics of free speech and activity.	Mentioned indirectly in over half of the grievances dealing with justice and legitimacy of decision making.
6. Efficiency of governmental operations.	Administrative structures that can efficiently deal with societal conditions.	Mentioned directly in one of the grievances and implicit in many of those dealings with the dissolution of legislature.
7. Equality	Rules and conditions that allow each individual the same opportunities as every other individual.	Not directly mentioned in the grievances but appears in the opening rhetoric.

a natural condition for most public policy issues, given the very
nature of public policy issues and the number of actors representing
different value perspectives. Both the definitions and the ranking
of values are difficult to establish. This is true even when there
is general agreement on the issue, as there was in the case of the
Declaration. Nevertheless, in order to perform systematic evaluation, such agreement must be assumed.

Therefore, to complete the first step in systematic evaluation, it is necessary to clearly define and establish priorities
for the major value concerns. Such a listing is assumed to be
correct for purposes of the evaluation, although disagreement may
be present.

2. Measuring the Values

Assuming you have defined and ordered values, the next step is
to evaluate the degree to which the values are maximized by conditions emanating from the public policy, or by the processes through
which the public policy is formulated and implemented. The task is
difficult because it involves determining empirical or real-world
indicators for each of the values, and then collecting samples of
data for those indicators that allow judgements to be made.

The determination of empirical indicators is called operationalization by social scientists. In the Declaration, the authors'
grievances could be considered rough operationalizations of the
values, since they were attempts to provide empirical information
on the degree to which certain values were achieved or threatened.
However, today's social scientists would not consider them to be
fully adequate operationalizations because the values were not
clearly defined and related to empirical conditions.

Crucial to good operationalization is the maxim that two or
more different people could take the definition and rules for
collecting the information and apply them to the real world with
the same results. The Declaration does not contain the rules for
operationalization, so it is very possible that a different set of
authors or even the same authors, a month later, would devise a
different list of grievances. Systematic evaluation requires that
data be collected according to specific rules guarding against
bias, as discussed under monitoring.

For example, you could operationalize the value of legitimacy
of the decision-making processes, by saying that the average length
and frequency of one colony's legislative meetings during the
1760s, represent a standard against which the length and frequency of the same meetings during the 1770s can be measured.
Once the norms are established and the procedures for measuring
the length and frequency delineated, you could measure the degree

to which the norm was violated in the 1770s.   This could be established for each colony, and would provide a picture of that particular aspect of legitimate decision-making process that would be the same, regardless of who collected the data.

However, even if such rules are developed and followed, the systematic evaluation of public policy issues requires that conditions be monitored to generate information allowing for comparison. The example above does allow for such a comparison because it creates the opportunity to measure a more stable period -- the 1760s -- with a period when it was asserted that illegitimate decision-making processes were fostered by the King.

There are two basic methods of generating comparative information. One method frequently used in public policy issue analysis is the monitoring of conditions over a period of time, referred to as <u>longitudinal analysis</u>. This method's ability to trace a condition in the policy environment prior to, and after the initiation of a policy, accounts for its frequent use. The second method, <u>cross-sectional analysis</u>, entails the collection of information used to compare units experiencing similar conditions. For example, the British decisions regarding the American colonies during the decades 1760-1780 could be compared with treatment of other British colonies during that same time period. This would help to ascertain the degree of difference in the decision-making processes.

Table 1.7 summarizes the guidelines for evaluation presented.

TABLE 1.7:   Summary of Guidelines for Evaluating
             Public Policy Issues

---

1. Clearly define relevant values -- self-interest and public
    interest.

2. Establish priorities among values so that the most important
    can be evaluated.

3. Develop rules for collecting information relevant to those
    values (operationalization).

4. Collect data that allow for comparisons over time or across
    similar situations or both.

D.   Prescription

Prescription is the suggestion and assessment of alternative public policies, and builds on the three forms of analysis already discussed. It requires that existing conditions be monitored and evaluated and that future conditions be predicted. Because it incorporates all three forms of analysis, prescription is the most complicated of the four types of analysis.

The difficulties inherent in the task of prescription are illustrated by the Declaration of Independence. That document announces the establishment of a free and independent United States of America as the prescription for all of the colonies' ills discussed in the document's body. It is clear from the wording of the document that though the authors felt the establishment was the only logical course of action, they were also aware that the course was both unpredictable and dangerous. Lack of certainty about outcome and the ratio of benefits to costs led the authors to end the Declaration in a manner that can only be interpreted as anxious desperation. This is illustrated by the statement, "And for the support of this Declaration, with a firm reliance on the protection of Divine Providence, we mutually pledge to each other our Lives, our Fortunes and our sacred Honour."

While most public policy issues do not raise such massive uncertainties and monumental costs as did the Declaration of Independence, they all confront political actors with uncertainties regarding costs and benefits. For that reason, it is necessary when approaching a prescription to provide information on the relative benefits and costs of alternative solutions to the public policy issues. To obtain such information, one must build on monitoring, forecasting, and evaluating.

If you employ systematic monitoring information, it is possible to form a base line against which policy can be forecasted and evaluated. The evaluation of an existing public policy issue can indicate the degree to which the important values were maximized under the present policy. A forecast assuming the continuation of the same policy could indicate the likely benefits and costs, given those values in future perspective. Against these projections, one can estimate the degree to which alternatives would be "better" or "worse" than the continuation of the correct policy.

A policymaker constructing the Declaration today would possibly have collected data on trade patterns involving the colonies, and then projected the likely future patterns of the colonies if they continued under the existing regime. Then, alternative arrangements could have been identified. Each of the alternatives could have been analyzed with forecasts made of the determined consequences. Finally, a comparison could have been made between the consequences,

of alternative policies and the continued control by Great Britain.
A graph similar to Figure 1.4 could be developed which provided
alternative projections. We use alternative dotted lines to
represent different projections. This type of graph represents
the previously discussed systematic prescriptive analysis.

Figure 1.4:   Alternative Projections of
Total Imports and Exports

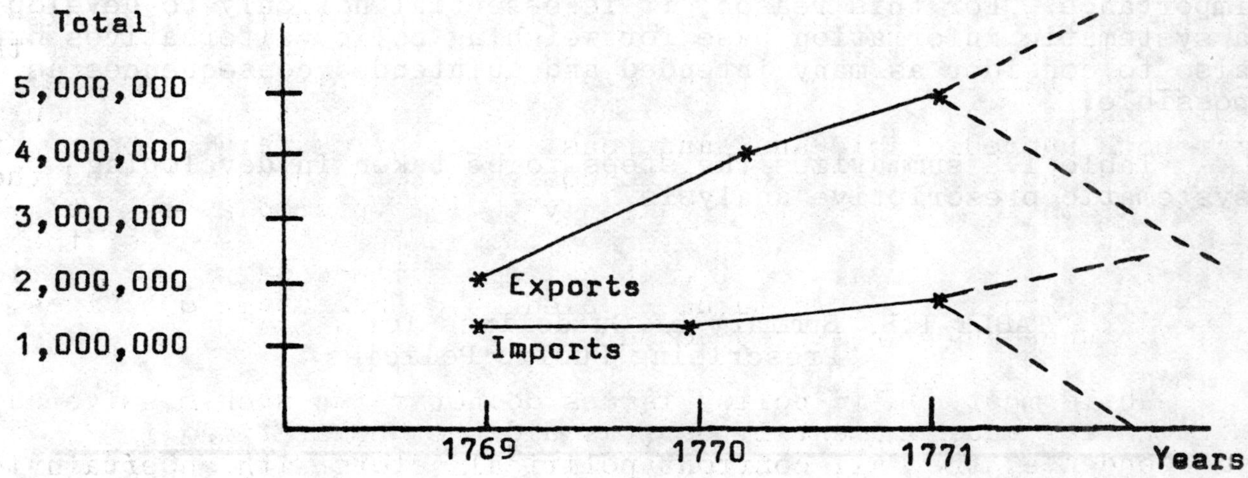

Source: Oliver M. Dickerson, The Navigation Acts and
the American Revolution, Philadelphia:
University of Pennsylvania, 1951.

While it is important to attempt to develop a systematic basis
for such prescriptions, as illustrated by our example, it is also
important to attempt to measure both the intended and unintended
consequences of a given public policy alternative. It is true that
one course of action might raise trade for the colonies, but what
additional costs and benefits would result? Frequently, those
costs and benefits cannot be easily measured in quantitative terms.
There are a variety of methods for estimating costs and benefits
and in fact there is an entire set of procedures frequently called
cost-benefit analysis. However, it is sometimes impossible to
estimate such costs or benefits.

For example, how do you estimate the amount of life and property destroyed by the War of Independence? Was the establishment

of the United States more costly than the continuation of British rule would have been? How do you take into account the effect of time on the policy alternative? The generation living at the time of the War for Independence suffered more of the costs than the next generation, while the latter no doubt enjoyed more of the benefits. In such areas as security from invasions by foreign powers or limitations on the flow of people between Britain and the United States, it is possible that independence was more costly for individuals in the colonies.

As stated earlier, these areas of assessment are more complicated than some of the public policy issues that confront us today. However, these kinds of considerations are of extreme importance. For this reason, it is essential not only to develop a systematic information base for weighing policy alternatives but also to consider as many intended and unintended consequences as possible.

Table 1.8 summarizes the steps to be taken in developing systematic prescriptive analysis.

TABLE 1.8   Summary of Guidelines for
Prescribing Public Policies

---

1. Conduct a systematic monitoring, forecasting, and evaluation of existing public policy.

2. Identify alternatives and project their consequences.

3. List all possible intended and unintended consequences.

4. Weigh the benefits and costs of the consequences of each of the alternatives including the continuation of the existing policy, as much as possible.

EXERCISE 1.3: Applying the Four Types of Analysis

Select an editorial that takes a position on a public policy issue. Identify one of each of the four types of analysis expressed in the editorial either by quoting directly from the editorial or paraphrasing what was said. After you have listed each of the four statements, write a brief essay assessing the analysis presented in the editorial using the criteria provided in this chapter.

APPENDIX I: Rules for the Good Society Exercise

You are about to participate in a society consisting of seven teams. Six of the teams consist of two to five players each and are called Groups (A, B, C, D, E, F). The other team consists of four to six players and is called the Central Authority. The Groups and the Central Authority behave in the Good Society according to the following statement of principle:

This society guarantees equal opportunity and equal rights to every member. It advocates the need for stability, change, and justice. Inequality is as enslaving as disorder. Order and justice must prevail.

Despite this statement of principle, the "goods" of the Good Society, as measured by Power Units, are not distributed equally. Moreover, the ability to make changes in the Good Society are not shared equally by the groups. The simulation exercise is designed to represent what happens in a society in which order and justice are its guidelines, yet the reality of the society runs counter to those guidelines.

Changes in the Good Society

Power Weights (the units used to measure the wealth and influence of each team in the society) and Petition Weights (the weight of each team in the signing of a Petition) are distributed in the following manner among the seven teams of the Good Society.

Name of Team	Power Weights	Petition Weights
Central Authority	100	3
Group A	45	2
Group B	35	2
Group C	10	1
Group D	8	1
Group E	4	1
Group F	4	1
Total	206	11

Changes in the distribution of power units as well as any other facet of life in the Good Society can occur in two ways:

.   A Petition can be signed by the teams representing at least six Petition Weights which call for any specific change.

.   A War can be fought between any team in the society in which the more powerful size (the larger number of Power Weights) gets all but one of the losing side's Power Weights.

In any redistribution of power point, no fractions may be used. Power points may be neither created or destroyed.

Maintaining Order in the Good Society

The maintenance of order in the Good Society is the responsibility of all of the members, although given the large number of Power Units at its disposal, the Central Authority has a special role. It can engage in War against members that fail to live up to the principles of the society and can attempt to get Petitions signed. At the same time, it is up to the six groups to make sure that the Central Authority does not abuse its role. These groups can sign Petitions to limit the actions of the Central Authority, even to the point of redistributing the power. (It is important to note that in any redistribution of power units, fractions cannot be used and power units cannot be destroyed or created.)

1. All decisions taken by the Groups must be unanimous. All decisions taken by Central Authority must be supported by a majority of all its members.

2. A Petition Form will be used for purposes of peaceful change. Any Group or the Central Authority can initiate a Petition. Once enough signatures of teams to constitute six Petition Weights has been achieved, the Petition should be submitted to Simulation Control. It goes into effect <u>as soon as Central officially announces the Petition</u>. It remains in effect until a different Petition is completed to alter the original one. No Petition can go into effect between the first declaration of War and the end of the War ten minutes later.

3. War occurs when one or more teams declares War against one or more other teams. A War Form is submitted to the Simulation Control, who will inform the other teams. The attacked team will have five minutes to counterattack. More than one team can attack and more than one can counterattack. The side with the largest number of Power Units will win the War and will get all but one of the other team's Power Units. If more than two teams attack and win, the power units won will be

distributed in accordance with the relative Power Units of the winning team. Any teams submitting a War Form may retract it before the five-minute time limit is up.

Familiarize yourself with the two types of forms which you will use in the game: <u>Petition Forms</u> and <u>War Forms</u>. Copies of each form will be available from Simulation Control.

PETITION FORM

CIRCLE THE INITIATOR: Central Authority A B C D E F
                              (Circle One)

OUTCOME CALLED FOR: ____

____

TEAM	PETITION WEIGHTS	SIGNATURES
Central Authority	3	__________
Group A	2	__________
Group B	2	__________
Group C	1	__________
Group D	1	__________
Group E	1	__________
Group F	1	__________

(In order for the outcome to become a part of the Good Society,
enough teams representing at least six Petition Weights must
agree to the Petition. A majority of members of Central Authority must sign for its Petition Weights to count. All members
of any group must sign for its Petition Weights to count.)

WAR FORM

CIRCLE ATTACKER(S):   CENTRAL AUTHORITY   A B C D E F
                              (Circle One or More)

CIRCLE TARGET(S):   CENTRAL AUTHORITY   A B C D E F
                              (Circle One or More)

SIGNATURES OF EACH MEMBER OF ATTACKING TEAM

____

____

____

CHAPTER TWO: LIBRARY RESEARCH FOR THE ANALYSIS OF PUBLIC POLICY

THE PRIMARY OBJECTIVE:

To assist you in identifying and locating information
available in libraries on specific public policy issues.

UPON COMPLETION OF THIS CHAPTER, YOU WILL BE ABLE TO:

* Locate definitions for any terms related to a particular
  policy issue.

* Identify and locate descriptive information on events and
  conditions relevant to a public policy issue.

* Identify and locate appropriate books, articles, governmental and nongovernmental information for your public
  policy issue.

* Access information stored on microform as appropriate to
  your research.

(Based on PS-19: Library Research for the Analysis of Public Policy,
Renee S. Captor, Croton-on-Hudson, NY: Policy Studies Associates,
1979.)

I: INTRODUCTION

This chapter can be used in two ways: it can serve as a step-by-step guide in doing in-depth research on a specific topic, or as a general introduction to library research. The exercises in each section will give a better understanding of the way to use each type of information source, and are designed as an integral part of the learning process.

This chapter should improve your skills in researching topics which are <u>public policy issues</u> -- defined as those which concern governmental action on matters involving societal conditions, and over which people disagree. Before beginning, a public policy issue should be chosen. If you have a public policy issue in mind, then you are ready to begin working; if not, you might try one of the following:

1. CETA and other manpower policies.

2. A proposed constitutional amendment.

3. Urban Renewal.

4. Medicaid.

5. Controversial changes in the Juvenile Justice System.

EXERCISE 2.1: Choosing a Topic

My Proposed Topic Is ____

____

II: DEFINITIONS -- DICTIONARIES AND ENCYCLOPEDIAS

The first step in research is to clearly define what you are studying. Often, a close look at the definition of your topic will give a better idea of what types of facts are called for and where these facts might be found.

Occasionally, you might run across specialized terms, or "jargon." A dictionary or encyclopedia will supply a definition that could clarify these specialized terms, allowing a better understanding of technical writings.

DICTIONARIES

Dictionaries primarily give short definitions, proper spelling, pronunciation, and syllabification. Some dictionaries also provide information on the origin of the word. The following are some good, all-purpose dictionaries:

Morris, William ed., American Heritage Dictionary of the English Language, New York: American Heritage Publishing Co., 1969.

Murray, James A.H. et al., eds., The Oxford English Dictionary, Oxford: Clarendon Press, 1933 (with supplements).

Neilson, Allan, ed., Webster's New International Dictionary of the English Language, Springfield: G. & C. Merriam Co., 1961.

Stein, Jess, ed., The Random House Dictionary of the English Language, New York: Random House, 1966.

If you are looking for a specialized term, a more specialized dictionary might be necessary. You might try one of the following:

Gamboa, Melquiades, Dictionary of International Law and Diplomacy, Dobbs Ferry, NY: Oceana Publications, 1974.

Hold, Sol, ed., <u>Dictionary of American Government</u>,
New York: Manor Books, 1970.

Piano, Jack, and Milton Greenberg, <u>The American
Political Dictionary</u>, Hinsdale, IL: Dryden
Press, 1967.

Piano, Jack, and Roy Olton, <u>International Relations
Dictionary</u>, New York: Holt, Rinehart & Winston,
1979.

Raymond, Walter J. <u>Dictionary of Politics: Selected
American and Foreign Political and Legal Terms</u>,
Lawrenceville, VA: Hampton Institute Press, 1978.

Reading, Hugo, <u>Dictionary of the Social Science</u>,
Boston: Routledge & Keegan, 1977.

ENCYCLOPEDIAS

Encyclopedias define both terms and concepts, and give much broader definitions than dictionaries. Like the dictionaries, encyclopedias can be either general or specialized. Two good general encyclopedias are:

Cayne, Bernard, ed., <u>Encyclopedia Americana</u>, Danbury, CT:
Grolier Educational Corp., 1978. This 30-volume
work is particularly good for information on towns
and cities.

Preece, Warren, ed., <u>Encyclopaedia Britannica</u>, Chicago:
Encyclopaedia Britannica, 1979. Another 30-volume
work, recently revised in an attempt to make it easier
to use, this is the most famous encyclopedia in
English -- and for some purposes the best.

If you are looking for a more specialized definition, you might try:

DeConde, Alexander, <u>Encyclopedia of American Foreign Policy</u>,
New York: Charles Scribner's Sons, 1979. This
selective reference work contains especially
commissioned articles dealing with the formative
ideas of American foreign policy.

Sills, David, ed., <u>International Encyclopedia of the
Social Sciences</u>, New York: Macmillan, 1977. This
8-volume set was intended to complement its
predecessor, <u>Encyclopedia of the Social Sciences</u>.

Its primary focus is on the rapid developments
of the 1960s, with emphasis on the analytical
and comparative aspects of a topic.

EXERCISE 2.2: Dictionaries and Encyclopedias

Choose three terms pertaining to your public policy issue, and
list them under the proper heading. Then look up the first term
in a general encyclopedia, the second in a general dictionary, and
the third in a specialized dictionary or encyclopedia. Note titles
and definitions in the spaces provided.

Term 1: ____

General Encyclopedia Used: _______________________________

Definition: ____

Term 2: ____

General Dictionary Used: _________________________________

Definition: ____

Term 3: ____

Specialized Work Used: ___________________________________

Definition: ____

III: BACKGROUND INFORMATION -- JOURNAL ARTICLES

Now that you have clarified your topic, you are ready to begin researching it. The next step is to locate some background information on your public policy issue.

Journal articles can be used to provide both background information and more information on the current status of your public policy issue. Because of the huge number of articles published, a systematic method of access is needed -- through abstracting and indexing services. These sources serve as a listing of articles, most often by subject, and provide the article title, author, journal, date, issue, volume, and page number.

There are five kinds of indexes:

1. General indexes: These cover a number of periodicals on a number of subjects.

2. Subject indexes: These cover several periodicals on one general topic.

3. Single title indexes: These cover only one publication or title.

4. Newspaper indexes: Like the single title indexes, these sources cover only one title. Each index catalogues only one newspaper's offerings.

5. Abstracts: These indexes provide, in addition to the index information, brief summaries of the articles.

Indexes are arranged alphabetically by subject, and occasionally by author as well. Since it is likely that you will be conducting a search by subject, you will be faced with the problem of what subject headings to look under.

There are two sources that will help you locate the proper heading. The Library of Congress List of Subject Headings will provide the subject heading used by the Library of Congress in cataloguing materials. This source, however, gives only Library of Congress headings, which may differ from the headings in an index or abstracting source.

Another source that can be used is the <u>Cross Reference Index</u>. The <u>Cross Reference Index</u> lists the subject headings used by the Library of Congress, the <u>New York Times</u>, <u>Sears List of Subject Headings</u>, <u>Readers' Guide to Periodical Literature</u>, <u>Business Periodicals Index</u>, and <u>PAIS</u>.

Indexes can be found to cover almost any area of interest. For public policy purposes, however, you will be interested in those abstracts and indexes dealing with the Social Sciences.

GENERAL INDEXES

<u>Readers' Guide to Periodical Literature</u>, New York: H. W. Wilson Co., 1900-. This index provides a well-balanced guide to nontechnical journals. About 169 periodicals are catalogued.

SUBJECT INDEXES

<u>ABC Political Science: Advance Bibliography of Contents: Political Science and Government</u>, Santa Barbara, CA: ABC-Chicago, 1969-. A service listing the contents of the latest journals in the fields of political science, government, public policy, etc.

<u>Bulletin of the Public Affairs Information Service (PAIS)</u>, New York: PAIS, 1915-. This multi-volume set is a subject index to current literature on economic and social conditions.

<u>Business Periodicals Index</u>, New York: H. W. Wilson Co., 1958-. A service that indexes 170 periodicals in various fields of business and management.

<u>Education Index</u>, New York: H. W. Wilson Co., 1929-. This is a cumulative subject index to about 240 periodicals in the field of education.

<u>Index of Economic Articles in Journals and Collective Volumes</u>, Homewood, IL: R. D. Irwin Co., 1961-. The index lists articles from about 140 sources from various countries.

<u>Index to Current Urban Documents</u>, Westport, CT: Greenwood Press, 1972-. This source contains originally indexed federal, state, and local documents.

<u>Social Sciences Citation Index</u>, Philadelphia: Institute for
    Scientific Information, 1973-. An international inter-
    disciplinary index to the literature of the Social
    Sciences.

<u>ABSTRACTS</u>

<u>Abstracts on Criminology and Penology</u>, Amsterdam: Excerpta
    Criminologica Foundation, 1961-. An abstract journal of
    literature related to criminology.

<u>Dissertation Abstracts International</u>, Ann Arbor, MI:
    University Microfilms, 1938-. Abstracts of doctoral
    dissertations in three volumes: Humanities and Social
    Sciences, Science and Engineering, and European Abstracts.

<u>Human Resources Abstracts</u>, Beverly Hills, CA: Sage Publica-
    tions, 1975-. This covers material related to social and
    manpower problems.

<u>International Political Science Abstracts</u>, Oxford: Inter-
    national Political Science Association, 1932-. A source
    which covers articles in the field of political science.

<u>Journal of Economic Literature</u>, Cambridge, MA: Harvard
    University, 1969-. This source contains lengthy
    abstracts from 35 journals. (Formerly <u>Journal of
    Economic Abstracts</u>.)

<u>Psychological Abstracts</u>, Lancaster, PA: American Psychological
    Association, 1927-. An important bibliography, listing
    and abstracting new materials in the field.

<u>Sociological Abstracts</u>, New York: Sociological Abstracts,
    1952-. A classified abstracting journal that covers a
    broad range of topics of international interest.

<u>Women's Studies Abstracts</u>, Rush, NY: Rush Publishing Co.,
    1972-. This source contains abstracts from a broad
    range of periodicals dealing with topics concerning
    women.

EXERCISE 2.3: Finding Journal Articles

Part 1: Choose two abstracting or indexing services that could
be used to find articles on your topic, and list them below
in spaces provided. Under each source, list the subject
headings used in locating relevant articles.

Source 1: ______________________________________

Headings: ______________________________

____

Source 2: ______________________________________

Headings: ______________________________

____

Part 2: Give a one-paragraph summary of one of the articles.

IV: DESCRIPTIONS OF CONDITIONS -- ALMANACS, YEARBOOKS,
AND STATISTICAL SOURCES

Often, in addition to background information, you will find
it necessary to seek information on conditions in the policy
environment. This can usually be accomplished through statistical
data as well as general descriptive information.

Almanacs and yearbooks give both statistical and general
descriptive information in an easy-to-acquire format. Both sources
are extremely useful in acquiring information on environmental
conditions.

ALMANACS

Information Please Almanac, New York: Simon & Schuster,
1947-.

Reader's Digest Almanac, Pleasantville, NY: Reader's
Digest Association, 1969-.

The World Almanac and Book of Facts, New York: Newspaper
Enterprise Association, 1868-.

YEARBOOKS

American Foreign Relations, A Documentary Record, New York:
Harper & Row, 1921-.

The County Yearbook, Washington, DC: International City
Management Association, 1975-.

The Municipal Yearbook, Washington, DC: International City
Management Association, 1934-.

STATISTICAL SOURCES
=================

Council of the States, Book of the States, Lexington, KY:
The Council, 1935-.

U.S. Bureau of the Census, City Government Finances, Washington, DC: Government Printing Office, 1909-.

U.S. Bureau of the Census, County and City Data Book,
Washington, DC: Government Printing Office, 1949-.

U.S. Bureau of the Census, State Government Finances,
Washington, DC: Government Printing Office, 1915-.

U.S. Bureau of the Census, Statistical Abstract of the
U.S., Washington, DC: Government Printing Office,
1878-.

Wasserman, Paul, Eleanor Allen, and Charlotte Georgi,
Statistical Sources, 5th ed., Detroit: Gale
Research Co., 1977.

EXERCISE 2.4: Finding Statistics

Select three statistics related to your public policy issue.
On the next page, record them in the proper places on the chart.
Look up these statistics in one yearbook, one almanac, and one
other source. If the statistic appears in the source, then note
down the number; if not, then place a "0" in the cell. For
example, after looking up the number of states in the Information
Please Almanac and finding that there were 50, the number 50 would
be written in the row labeled "Information Please Almanac"
(Almanac Title), and under the statistical column entitled "number
of states."

	Statistic 1 Is:	Statistic 2 Is:	Statistic 3 Is:
Almanac Title:			
Yearbook Title:			
Other Source Title:			

V: EVENTS -- NEWSPAPERS AND SURVEYS OF EVENTS

Now that you have background information and information on conditions on your public policy issue, you can begin to delve into the specifics of your topic. Since your public policy issue is probably an item of current concern, the best places to find information on events are newspapers and surveys of events.

Every library will subscribe to at least one national newspaper, and most will subscribe to several. The larger national newspapers have indexes to the paper which will allow you to easily locate events pertaining to your topic.

In addition to newspapers, surveys of events provide information on recent happenings. These sources tend to give more information and often include some background information on the topic.

NEWSPAPER INDEXES

Christian Science Monitor Index, Boston: Christian Science Monitor, 1960-.

National Observer Index, Princeton, NJ: Dow Jones Books, 1971-.

Newspaper Index: The Chicago Tribune, The Los Angeles Times, The New Orleans Times -- Picayune, The Washington Post, Wooster, OH: Bell & Howell, 1972-.

Wall Street Journal Index, New York: Dow Jones & Co., 1958-.

SURVEYS OF EVENTS

Annual Register of World Events, London: Publisher varies, 1758-.

Congressional Index, Chicago: Commerce Clearinghouse, 1937-.

<u>Congressional Quarterly Weekly Report</u>, Washington, DC:
Congressional Quarterly, 1945-.

<u>Deadline Data on World Affairs</u>, Greenwich, CT: DMS, 1968-.

<u>Facts on File</u>, New York: Facts on File, 1940-.

EXERCISE 2.5: Finding Events

Using the <u>New York Times Index</u>, compile a list of three major
events. These events should be specific actions of legislation,
judicial decisions, or significant actions of large groups of
people. Record the date and page number of the <u>Times</u> article.
Next, look up the same three events in one other newspaper index and
one survey of events, and record the dates and pages of the articles.
Since often these articles do not appear on the same day, or even
within the same week, it is necessary to check the other sources
sometime earlier and sometime after the event. If the event does
not appear in the source, leave the box empty.

	Event 1:	Event 2:	Event 3:
<u>N.Y. Times</u> <u>Index</u>	Date: Page No:	Date: Page No:	Date: Page No:
Newspaper Index #2:	Date: Page No:	Date: Page No:	Date: Page No:
Survey of Events #1:	Date: Page No:	Date: Page No:	Date: Page No:

VI: INFORMATION THROUGH DOCUMENTS -- U.S. GOVERNMENT
PUBLICATIONS

Every year the United States government publishes thousands
of pages of material on many different subjects. These materials
can be very valuable in studying public policy issues.

Before you can locate documents on your subject, it is
essential to identify the agency associated with your topic, since
most government documents are authored by agencies and not individuals. The United States Government Manual clearly outlines the
purposes and structures of most agencies and departments.

Perhaps the most important book in your search is the Monthly
Catalog of the United States Government Publications. If you
know the agency associated with your topic, simply refer to the
author index in the back of the Monthly Catalog under that agency
and endeavor to locate any pertinent titles. The "List of Government Authors" at the beginning of the Catalog will tell you on
which page number the entries for your agency begin. If you are
not sure what agency is associated with your topic, or if there are
several agencies involved, you might wish to check the subject
index to publications in the Monthly Catalog. There is also a title
index if you are searching for a specific title.

Among other details, each entry in the Monthly Catalog gives
the entry number, the author, the title, the date, and the Superintendent of Documents (Su-Doc) number.

Documents may be arranged in your library in two ways -- either
catalogued by government author and shelved along with other books,
or arranged according to Su-Doc number and catalogued by the
Monthly Catalog. Consult the librarian on how the collection is
organized.

Should more information on government documents be needed,
check: Joe Morehead, United States Public Documents (2nd ed.,
Littleton, CO: Libraries Unlimited, 1978).

List of Government Authors

	Beginning entry
Administrative Office of United States Courts, Washington, DC 20544	Ju 10.14:976
Aging Administration, Washington, DC 20201	HE 1.202:H 81
Agricultural Research Service, Washington, DC 20250	A 77.15:H-5-1,2
Agriculture Department, Washington, DC 20250	A 1.2:H 81/2
Air Force Department, Washington, DC 20330	D 301.85:1
Alcohol, Tobacco and Firearms Bureau, Washington, DC 20224	T 70.2:Al 1
Animal and Plant Health Inspection Service, Washington, DC 20250	A 101.10/2:91-31
Army Department, Washington, DC 20310	D 101.11:5-809-12
Assistant Public Printer (Superintendent of Documents) Government Printing Office, Washington, DC 20402	GP 3.9:36/160-161
Automated Data and Telecommunications Service, Washington, DC 20405	GS 12.13:976-77
Census Bureau, Suitland, MD 20233	C 3.6/2:C 33/6
Center for Disease Control, Atlanta, GA 30333	HE 20.7002:En 8/2
Central Intelligence Agency, Washington, DC 20505	PrEx 3.10:En 2
Child Development Office, Washington, DC 20201	HE 1.408:H 34
Civil Rights Commission, Washington, DC 20425	CR 1.2:C 49/5/976
Civil Service Commission, Washington, DC 20415	CS 1.2:Ag 8/2
Coast Guard, Washington, DC 20590	TD 5.2:St 5
Commissions, Committees, and Boards	Y 3.Ad 6:1/974-75
Community Health Services Bureau, Rockville, MD 20852	HE 20.5102:Ir 6
Community Relations Service, Washington, DC 20530	J 23.1:975
CONGRESS	
Congressional Serial Set	94:Cong.Serial
Laws	94.2:Pub.Law 469
American Indian Policy Review, Commission on, Washington, DC 20515	Y 4.In 2/10:F 31
Congressional Budget Office, Washington, DC 20515	Y 10.2:Ad 9/2
Congressional Operations, Joint Committee on, Washington, DC 20515	Y 4.C 76/7:C 83/976
Economic Joint Committee, Washington, DC 20510	Y 4.Ec 7:F 73/5/970-74
House of Representatives, Washington, DC 20515	
House documents	94-1:H.doc.118
House reports	95-1:H.rp.76
Aging, Select Committee on, Washington, DC 20515	Y 4.Ag 4/2:El 2/12
Agriculture, Committee on, Washington, DC 20515	Y 4.Ag 8/1:M 66/3
Appropriations, Committee on, Washington, DC 20515	Y 4.Ap 6/1:Ag 8/978/pt.2-7
Armed Services, Committee on, Washington, DC 20515	Y 4.An 5/2 a:977-78/10
Banking, Finance and Urban Affairs, Committee on, Washington, DC 20515	Y 4.B 22/1:Ex 7/10/977
Budget, Committee on the, Washington, DC 20515	Y 4.B 85/3:En 2/2/978
Education and Labor, Committee on, Washington, DC 20515	Y 4.Ed 8/1:R 26/3
Government Operations, Committee on, Washington, DC 20515	Y 4.G 74/7:Ac 2/8
Interior and Insular Affairs, Committee on, Washington, DC 20515	Y 4.In 8/14:94-5/pt.2
International Relations, Committee on, Washington, DC 20515	Y 4.In 8/16:H 88/17
Interstate and Foreign Commerce, Committee on, Washington, DC 20515	Y 4.In 8/4:Ai 7/34/977
Judiciary, Committee on the, Washington, DC 20515	Y 4.J 89/1:94-49
Merchant Marine and Fisheries, Committee on, Washington, DC 20515	Y 4.M 53.95-A
Post Office and Civil Service, Committee on, Washington, DC 20515	Y 4.P 84/10:F 31 p/975
Public Works and Transportation, Committee on, Washington DC 20515	Y 4.P 96/11:95-3
Science and Technology, Committee on, Washington, DC 20515	Y 4.Sci 2:94-2/WW
Veterans' Affairs, Committee on, Washington, DC 20515	Y 4.V 64/3:M 46/10/975
Ways and Means, Committee on, Washington, DC 20515	Y 4.W 36:D 71/2/974
Senate, Washington, DC 20510	Y 1.95/1:E
Senate documents	94-1:S.doc.117
Senate reports	95-1:S.rp.30
Agriculture, Nutrition, and Forestry, Committee on, Washington, DC 20510	Y 4.Ag 8/3:W 58
Agriculture and Forestry, Committee on, Washington, DC 20510	Y 4.Ag 8/2:Ag 8/24/977
Appropriations, Committee on, Washington, DC 20510	Y 4.Ap 6/2:Ec 7/3/977
Armed Services, Committee on, Washington, DC 20510	Y 4.Ar 5/3:D 61

SAMPLE ENTRY

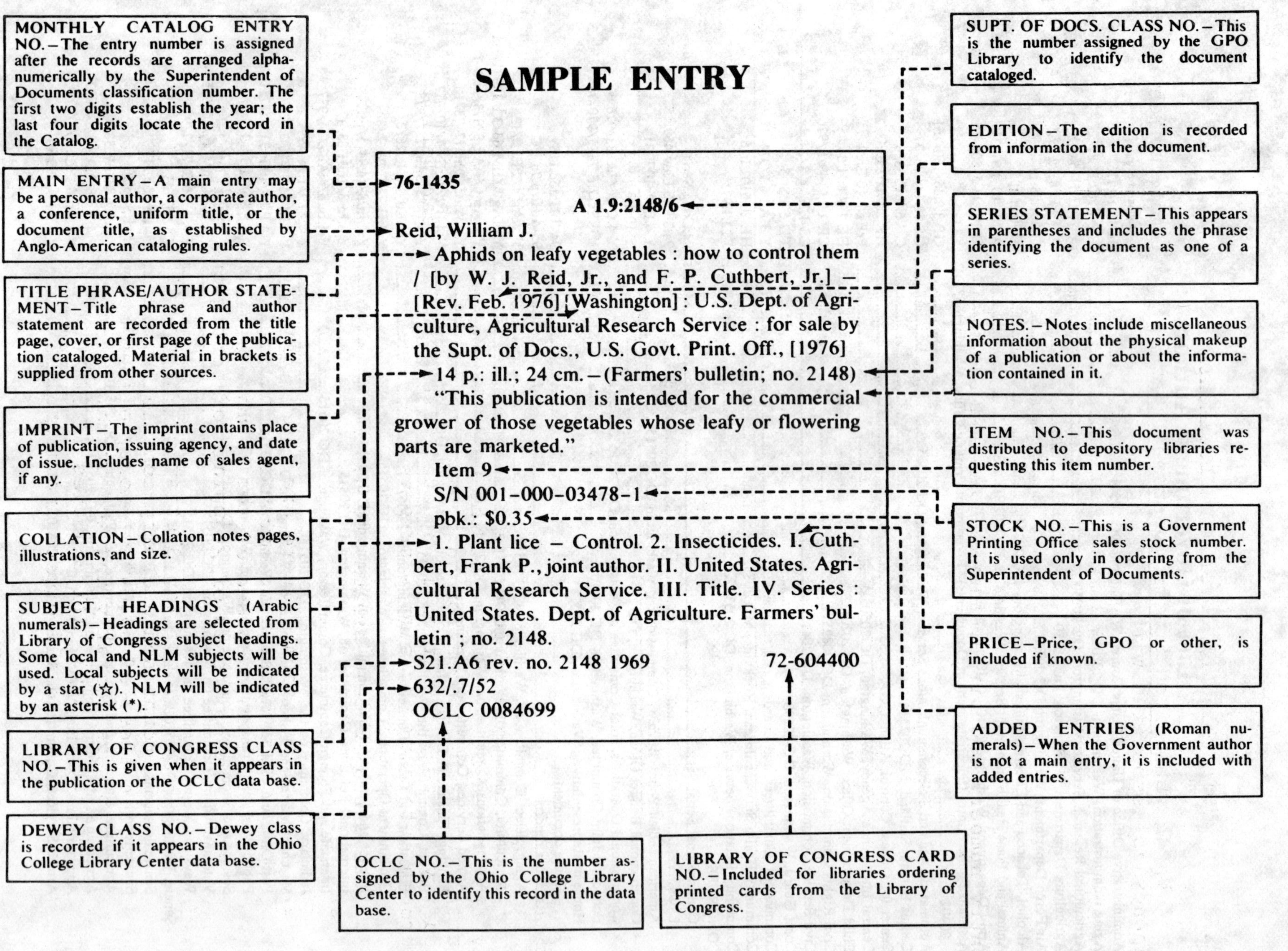

EXERCISE 2.6a: Finding Government Documents

Using the <u>United States Government Manual</u>, determine which agency is associated with your topic.

My Agency Is ____

Using the <u>Monthly Catalog of United States Government Publications</u>, locate three publications relevant to your topic and give the entry number, the title, the author, and the Su-Doc number.

1. ____

    ____

2. ____

    ____

3. ____

    ____

<u>CENSUS DATA</u>

A special type of government document is information published by the United States Bureau of the Census. Every 10 years the Bureau collects information on population and housing for the entire country. This information is updated within the 10-year period through estimated and sample surveys.

The Census Bureau breaks the nation down in several ways. These are:

1. Regions/Division. There are four census regions (west, south, northeast, and north central) defined for the United States, each composed of two or more divisions. Divisions are areas composed of groupings of contiguous states.

2. Standard Metropolitan Statistical Areas (SMSAs). In 1970, an SMSA comprised a county containing a central city (or twin cities) of 50,000 or more, plus contiguous counties which were socially and economically integrated with the central county. All counties in SMSAs are termed "metropolitan," and all others "nonmetropolitan."

3. Urbanized Areas (UAs). UAs comprise a central city of an SMSA, plus the surrounding closely settled urban fringe ("suburbs").

4. Urban/Rural. The urban population comprises all persons living in urbanized areas and in places of 2,500 or more outside urbanized areas. Everyone else is considered rural.

5. Unincorporated Places. A concentration of population which is not legally incorporated. Suitable boundaries are defined for statistical purposes by the Census Bureau with local assistance. Unincorporated places of less than 1,000 inhabitants are disregarded.

6. Census Tracts. Subdivisions of SMSAs averaging 4,000 population, covering all SMSAs for 1970. Tracts are defined by local committees and are frequently used to approximate neighborhoods.

7. Enumeration Districts (EDs). Administrative divisions set up by the Census Bureau to take the census in areas where enumerators were used, averaging 800 population. Outside of urbanized areas, this is the smallest geographic unit of analysis, and all other areas (tracts, places, MCDs, etc.) can be defined as a collection of EDs.

8. Block Groups (BGs). Groups of city blocks, averaging 1,000 population, which take the place of enumeration districts in 145 large urbanized areas where the census was taken by mail in 1970.

9. Blocks. City blocks are areas generally bounded by four streets or some other physical boundary, defined in urbanized areas and in additional cities which contracted with the Bureau for collection of block statistics.

The Census Bureau gathers information on many items under the two main headings of population and housing. Information includes:

Population Items

Relationship to head of household	Age
	Sex
Color or race	Marital Status

Housing Items

Number of housing units at this address	Flush toilet
Telephone	Bathtub or shower
Complete kitchen facilities	Owner/renter
Rooms	Commercial establishment on property
Water supply	Value

The information gathered is compiled in a series of reports covering a variety of areas and subjects. To find a specific subject the best source is <u>Index to Selected 1970 Census Reports</u>. A general guide to the rise of census data is the <u>1970 Census User's Guide</u>. Both of these publications are available from the Data User Services Division, U.S. Bureau of the Census, Washington, D.C.

EXERCISE 2.6b: Using Census Data

Choose an SMSA (Standard Metropolitan Statistical Area), perhaps the area in which you live.

My SMSA Is ____

Using a <u>Census Tract</u> report for this SMSA, locate the following information for your SMSA. (Table number is given.)

	Table Number	Data	
1.	P-1	Total Population	______
2.	P-1	Percent Negro	______
3.	P-1	Number of Persons 65 and Over	______
4.	P-1	Average Number of Persons Per Household	______
5.	P-4	Median Family Income	______
6.	P-4	Percent of Families Below Poverty Level	______

In completing this exercise, be sure to use the SMSA statistics, not the tract statistics.

VII.   INFORMATION TOOL -- USING MICROFORMS

In your search thus far, you have probably encountered micro-forms. In order to save space, back issues of many newspapers, some periodicals, and numerous U.S. government and international documents are put onto microforms. This process makes it possible for a library to hold much more in the way of past issues, and provides a way to keep material without having to worry about the decay or destruction of the printed material through age or constant use.

There are several types of microforms:

1. Microfilm: Microfilm is a reel of film, usually 100 feet (30m) long and 16mm or 35mm wide, containing photo copies of the material. It is the standard format for back-runs of journals.

2. Microfiche: Microfiche is a piece of exposed film, usually 4 inches by 6 inches, containing either 60 or 98 frames or pictures on a card in a grid pattern.

3. Micro-opaque: Because of the cost and difficulty of manufacture, these microforms are becoming obsolete. Micro-opaque is an opaque card with information printed on both sides. Unlike microfilm and microfiche, micro-opaque is read by reflecting light off the surface rather than shining light through it.

    a) Microcard: Microcard is a 3 inch-by-5 inch piece of micro-opaque.

    b) Microprint: Microprint cards are 9 inch-by-6 inch micro-opaques.

If you are interested in acquiring further information on microforms, you might try the following:

<u>Dissertation Abstracts International</u>, Ann Arbor, MI: University Microfilms, 1939-. Catalogues and abstracts doctoral dissertations.

<u>National Register of Microform Masters</u>, Washington, DC:
  Library of Congress, 1970-. Catalogues all material
  except newspapers and theses.

<u>Newspapers in Microform</u>, Washington, DC: Library of Congress,
  1970-. Catalogues all newspapers on microforms.

EXERCISE 2.7: Microforms

  Using a newspaper index such as the <u>New York Times</u>, locate an
article that provides either historical or general background
information on your topic. Have this article reproduced onto
paper and attach it to your paper.

VIII: IN-DEPTH INFORMATION -- LOCATING BOOKS

While much of the information you require for your research can be found in journals and newspapers, often you will find a need for more in-depth, detailed information. The best source is books.

Locating books in a library can be difficult, but if you acquaint yourself with the system of organization in your library, the job becomes much easier. At present there are two major coding systems for organizing a library collection, the Dewey Decimal System and the Library of Congress System.

The Dewey System divides all books into 10 major categories, each category bearing a number.

The major divisions are:

000 - General Works

100 - Philosophy and Related Disciplines

200 - Religion

300 - The Social Sciences

400 - Language

500 - Pure Sciences

600 - Technology (Applied Sciences)

700 - The Arts

800 - Literature and Rhetoric

900 - General Geography and History and Their Auxiliaries
            (including biography)

Each of these categories can be divided into 10 more sub-divisions. Since we are dealing primarily with the Social Sciences, it is useful to know how the Dewey System breaks down the 300 category:

300 - General	350 - Public Administration
310 - Statistics	360 - Welfare
340 - Law	370 - Education
320 - Political Science	380 - Commerce
330 - Economics	390 - Customs and Folklore

Under the Library of Congress System, the books are coded by a combination of numbers and letters. The first letter (or just two letters) denotes the subject heading.

The classifications are:

A - General Works and Polygraphy

B - Philosophy and Religion

C - Universal History

E-F - American History

G - Geography and Anthropology

H - Social Sciences

J - Political Science

K - Law

L - Education

M - Music

N - Fine Arts

P-O - Language and Literature

Q - Science

R - Medicine

S - Agriculture

T - Technology

U - Military Science

V - Naval Science

Z - Bibliography and Library Science

By knowing these classification systems, you can tell to some extent, by looking at the number, what the book is about and whether useful to you.

The first step in looking for books is to determine what the code on the book is. This is done through the card catalogue.

The card catalogue generally contains at least three cards for every book in a library collection -- title card, author card, and subject card. For the most part, these cards contain the same information, but are filed differently in the alphabetically ordered catalogue.

Each card contains information on title, author(s) or editor, place and date of publication, number of pages, size, contents, call number, and tracings. The tracings indicate other subject headings under which this book is located, and can also lead to additional titles on the same subject. Some books have tracings on all three cards, but others list tracings only on the author card.

The card catalogue will be one of two types, divided or nondivided. The divided catalogue will have author and title cards in the same file, with the subject cards filed separately. The nondivided dictionary catalogue will have all three types of cards indexed together in the same file.

The best place to begin your search is under the subject. You know what your topic is, and what subjects may be related. Go to the subject part of the catalogue and look up your subject. If you cannot find a related subject listed in the card catalogue, check the <u>Library of Congress List of Subject Headings</u>.

Once you have identified the book you want in the card catalogue, you must locate it on the shelf. Note the <u>call number</u> in the upper left corner of the card which is the code, either Dewey or Library of Congress, for your book. Then proceed to the stacks, arranged numerically for the Dewey and alpha-numerically for the Library of Congress, and locate your book.

EXERCISE 2.8: Books

Part 1: Using the system described above, locate and list three books related to your topic and give full bibliographical citation.

For example: Coplin, William D., and Michael K. O'Leary, <u>Everyman's PRINCE</u>, North Scituate, MA: Duxbury Press, 1972.

1. _______________________________

   ____

   ____

2. _______________________________

   ____

   ____

3. _______________________________

   ____

   ____

**Part 2: Give a brief summary of what information on your topic
two of these books would provide.**

IX: THE LEGAL SIDE -- USING THE LAW LIBRARY

A.   Legal Dictionaries

     Often when dealing with a public policy issue, you will wish
to check into the policy aspect of your topic by researching in a
law library. Before the law library can be effectively used, it
must be determined how certain facets of your topic are defined
under the law. To accomplish this, a specialized legal dictionary
should be consulted which will supply legal definitions of words
and phrases.

     Two good legal dictionaries are:

Ballantine's Law Dictionary with Pronunciations (William
     Anderson, ed.), Rochester, NY: Lawyers Co-operative
     Publishing Co., 1969.

Black's Law Dictionary, St. Paul, MN: West Publishing Co.,
     1968.

EXERCISE 2.9a: Legal Dictionaries

     Select one broad term or concept related to your public policy
issue. Look it up in a legal dictionary and identify the dictionary used.

Term: ____

Definition: ____

Dictionary: ____

B.   <u>Legal Periodicals</u>

A good starting point in becoming acquainted with the laws
governing your topic is to check legal periodicals. These contain
articles by established scholars, student comments, and case notes,
reflecting analysis of changes in the law as well as historical
developments.

To gain access to law journal articles, check the <u>Index to
Legal Periodicals</u>. This source indexes over 350 periodicals by
author, subject, cases, and book reviews.

EXERCISE 2.9b: Legal Periodicals

Part 1: Using the <u>Index to Legal Periodicals</u>, locate two journal
         articles on your topic and give the full citations:

         Article 1: ____

                     ____

                     ____

         Article 2: ____

                     ____

                     ____

Part 2: Locate a copy of one of the articles and write a brief
         summary below.

C.   Statutes

In order to find "the law," you must have some understanding of governmental organization. Our government is composed of three branches, each of which effect the law in their own way.

The legislative branch of government, the United States Congress determines what the laws should be. A statute is a law that has been passed by a legislature and written down.

The federal statutes are found in the U.S. Code, an official source issued by the United States Government Printing Office. Unfortunately, this source can run up to two years behind schedule.

Two more up-to-date, albeit unofficial, sources are U.S. Codes Annotated, a West publication, and U.S. Code Service, a Lawyers Co-operative publication. Better indexed and much easier to use, both sources are indexed by subject, include case references, and are updated at least once a year.

EXERCISE 2.9c: Finding Statutes

Using U.S. Code Annotated or U.S. Code Service, locate a federal statute in any way related to your topic. Give the title and volume number in which your statute appears, and the date the law was enacted.

The Title Is ____.

Section Number ______________. Date of Enactment ____________.

D.   U.S. Supreme Court Cases

The judicial branch of government judges people under the law and, through the U.S. Supreme Court, can decide the shape the law will take. For this reason, you will want to check on Supreme Court decisions in your topic area.

The official court reports are published as United States Reports. Two unofficial sources of Supreme Court decisions are Supreme Court Reporter (West Publishing Co.), and Lawyer's Edition of the U.S. Supreme Court Reports (Lawyers Co-operative). These are indexed by subject in two unofficial publications entitled Supreme Court Digest (West) and Digest of the U.S. Supreme Court

<u>Reports</u> (Lawyers Co-operative). These sources render citations in an easy-to-use form.

EXERCISE 2.9d: Locating Supreme Court Cases

Part 1: Using the <u>Supreme Court Digest</u> or <u>Digest of the U.S. Supreme Court Reports</u>, locate a decision by the Supreme Court related to your topic area. With the citation information you find, identify the case in the <u>United States Reports</u>, the <u>Supreme Court Reporter</u>, or the <u>Lawyer's Edition of the U.S. Supreme Court Reports</u>. Give the name of the case and the date it was decided.

    Name of Case: ____

    Date Decided: ____
    (Day, month, year)

Part 2: Write a short summary of what the case was about.

E.   <u>Administrative Regulations</u>

The third branch of government, the executive branch, sometimes legislates through federal agencies. An agency will issue rules and regulations to control a certain program or to enforce a law; these regulations have the force of law.

The <u>Code of Federal Regulations (CFR)</u>, a compilation of all federal rules and regulations, contains information about the organization of agencies, as well as the rules and regulations issued by an agency.

The daily supplement to the <u>CFR</u> is entitled the <u>Federal Register</u>. A rule or regulation cannot be enforced until it is published in the <u>Federal Register</u> which contains proposed regulations, notices, and amended rules and regulations for administrative agencies.

EXERCISE 2.9e: Locating Regulations

Part 1: Identify the federal administrative agency associated with your topic. Using the index to the <u>Code of Federal Regulations,</u> locate the volume in which many of your agency's rules and regulations appear.

The Volume Is ____

Part 2: Using a recent issue of the <u>Federal Register</u>, identify a proposed regulation, a notice, or an amended rule or regulation concerning your agency. Should additional information be needed, check two books by Morris L. Cohen, <u>Legal Research in a Nutshell</u>, 2nd ed. and <u>How To Find the Law</u>, 7th ed. (St. Paul, MN: West Publishing Co., 1971 and 1976). Describe below.

X: THE FINAL RESOURCE -- USING BIBLIOGRAPHIES

A final source in your search for information is the bibliography, defined as lists of materials in given subject areas. Bibliographies can be very broad or very specific. Besides books, there are bibliographies of magazines, newspapers, government publications, and microform.

A few examples of bibliographies in the public policy area are:

Besterman, Theodore, <u>Bibliography, Including Library Science and Reference Books</u>, Totawa, NJ: Rowman and Littlefield, 1971.

Bogdanor, V.B., <u>Bibliography for Students of Politics</u>, Fairlawn, NJ: Oxford University Press, 1971.

Delupis, Ingrid, <u>Bibliography of International Law</u>, New York: R. R. Bowker Co., 1976.

Sheehy, Eugene, <u>A Guide to Reference Books</u>, Chicago: American Library Association, 1976.

Unesco International Committee for Social Science Documentation, <u>International Bibliography of Economics</u>, Vol. 1, Chicago: Aldine Publishing Co., 1952-.

Unesco International Committee for Social Science Documentation, <u>International Bibliography of Political Science</u>, Vol. 1, Chicago: Aldine Publishing Co., 1952-.

Unesco International Committee for Social Science Documentation, <u>International Bibliography of Sociology</u>, Vol. 1, Chicago: Aldine Publishing Co., 1952-.

EXERCISE 2.10: Using Bibliographies

Locate three titles that might be of value for your topic. Note which bibliography was used and supply full citations for the books found.

The Bibliography Used Was ____

____

      Title 1: ____

               ____

      Title 2: ____

               ____

      Title 3: ____

               ____

CHAPTER THREE: INTRODUCTION TO SURVEYS AND INTERVIEWS

THE PRIMARY OBJECTIVE:

> To introduce the student to the concepts and skills used
> to conduct a sample survey.

UPON COMPLETION OF THIS CHAPTER, YOU WILL BE ABLE TO:

* Plan a simple sample survey.

* Identify various designs used to collect data.

* Identify various sampling procedures.

* Define and apply basic survey concepts.

(Based on <u>PS-12: Introduction to Surveys and Interviews</u>, Lawrence
P. Clark, Croton-on-Hudson, NY: Policy Studies Associates, 1976.)

I. INTRODUCTION TO SURVEYS

Over the years, the sample survey has become a common part of the American culture. From the backwoods of Washington State to the urban centers of the East coast, surveys are used to collect data on all types of questions from all kinds of subjects. The Gallup or Harris polls are familiar indicators of public opinion. In an election year, America is constantly bombarded with the results of surveys showing that this candidate or that one is ahead in different parts of the country.

What then is a survey? A survey is a process of gathering information about a group of subjects in which direct contact is made with those subjects. The subjects of a survey could be people, organizations, communities, governmental bodies, etc. The typical survey uses such techniques as the questionnaire and interview schedules to obtain information from the subjects.

A sample survey is different from a census or a poll. In a sample survey, information is collected from a fraction of the total number of subjects who are chosen to represent the total. A census is a type of survey in which data is compiled on all the subjects of interest. The term "poll" is used to describe a survey dealing with public opinion concerning elections or other public issues.

The major power of a survey lies in its ability to provide answers to such questions as: Who does what? Why? How? How well? With what effect? Throughout this chapter, a fictitious survey on food will be used to illustrate various points. A sample survey could help to generate answers to one or more of the following questions concerning food:

1. What are the characteristics of vegetarians? Are some parts of the country more likely to have vegetarians than other regions of the country?

2. Why do some families like having meat with every meal? Why do some people choose to use margarine in place of butter?

3. How did families cope with the rising food costs of
    1973-74? How are the menus composed for each meal?

4. How well does the food stamp program work? How well
    did a local nutrition education program work?

5. What were the effects of the closing of a local super-
    market? What were the effects of the recent sugar
    shortage?

The answers to these questions allow the surveyor to make
statements concerning the subjects under observation, i.e., statements he hopes represent the opinions of the larger population of
subjects from which the sample was drawn. The surveyor might want
to use such statements as part of a study performing one or more of
the following types of analysis:

Description of the population: What characteristics do
the subjects in the survey have in common?

Causal explanation: Why did something happen the way it
did? Was the hypothesis put forth to explain the change
correct?

Prediction of future conditions: What can be expected to
happen next month, next year, or over the next decade?

Evaluation of social programs: Did the program accomplish
the goals for which it was designed? Was this particular
program an efficient way of reaching those goals?

Development of social indicators: How satisfied are certain
subgroups of the population? What is the current feeling
about the quality of life in the United States?

As you progress through this chapter, you will examine the
various stages in the design and conduct of a sample survey which
would help you to answer some of the questions posed on the previous pages.

II: DESIGNING A SAMPLE SURVEY

The design of a sample survey is a planned schedule for collecting and analyzing the data required to satisfy the research objectives. Most surveys will have one or more of the following research objectives in mind when they are being designed: explanation of the various factors composing an issue; explanation of the causes of an issue; testing hypotheses about an issue; predicting future trends or events related to an issue; and the development of social indicators.

Exploration

There are many situations where the researcher simply does not have enough knowledge about the issue to really know where to begin. He might be tempted to do a survey in which the bulk of the questions were of the form "What sorts of things aggravate you the most about this particular issue?" or, "What are the good points of this issue?" The problem with questions of this nature lies in the ability to interpret the answers received which will range from a monosyllabic response to a half-hour speech on "What is Wrong with the Country." It will be extremely difficult to make any statements about the population from which the sample is drawn. For these reasons the sample survey is not the most efficient instrument for exploratory research.

Description

The aim of descriptive surveys is to measure certain items such as food preferences, religious affiliation, income, or educational achievement. The description of certain phenomena of interest can fill in the background necessary to formulate other research objectives that the survey sponsor might consider investigating at a later date.

Causal Explanations

A survey aimed at measuring causal explanations attempts to explain why an event or situation happened the way it did and what factors influenced or caused the final outcome. To demonstrate a causal relationship between factors and outcomes, three conditions must be satisfied. First, the factors which the researcher believes cause the outcome and that outcome must be associated with each other. That is, when the causal factors are present, then the outcome must also be present, at least under certain definable circumstances. The second condition is that the presumed causal factors must occur before the reported outcome, or at a minimum, the outcome should not take place before the causal factors. The final condition that must be satisfied before a causal relationship can be established between factors and outcomes is the elimination of all other rival explanations for the reported outcome. When these three conditions have been met, the researcher has a case for believing that the factors he or she investigated did indeed cause the reported outcome. For example, the researcher might be interested in ascertaining if the cutback in a number of policemen due to budgetary pressures was responsible for the most recent increase in crime. Or he/she might want to know if the rapid rise in food prices over the last few years has caused a shift in the eating habits of Americans.

However, with sample surveys the researcher rarely can adequately satisfy all three conditions, particularly the last, and therefore must be especially careful when using a sample survey as a causal explanation of a phenomenon.

Testing Hypotheses

This research objective is closely related to causal explanation. In order to say that a factor influenced or caused a reported outcome, underlying assumptions must exist about their relationship. Those underlying assumptions are called hypotheses. A hypothesis is a statement whose truthfulness can be tested by empirical data. Hypotheses usually take the form of a statement expressing a causal relationship, for example, "a drop in the price of beef will cause a rise in the national rate of beef consumption." The statement "God is responsible for the events which happen in our daily lives" would not be a hypothesis, even though many people believe the statement, since it is not possible to determine if there is a God by using empirical data. The ability to formulate hypotheses is valuable in the planning and designing of surveys since it forces the researcher to think about just what he expects to find using the survey.

Evaluation

The evaluation of planned programs of intervention is an increasingly popular use to which surveys are put these days. For example, a local city government may want to know if a social program designed to change people's attitudes towards nutrition does in fact change their attitudes. A state government might want to know what changes should be made in an after-school cultural enrichment program so that more children would attend. In each case, the sample survey is one instrument that the sponsors could use to obtain the information they desire.

Designing a survey for evaluation involves making decisions about the objectives of the sponsoring agency. Evaluation research can be broken down into two broad categories related to the focus and the time frame of the evaluation. In summative research, the objective of the evaluation is to study the effects of the social program -- i.e., did it accomplish the goals it set out to achieve? In formative research, the evaluation is concerned with the ongoing process of the social program and methods of improvement. The evaluation of a nutrition program conducted by a local city government is an example of an evaluation concerned with effects, that is, the outcome of the program. A state evaluation of an educational enrichment program is an example of an evaluation which is directed toward the ongoing process of a program. Some evaluations assess only the short-term effects of the program while others are aimed at the program's long-term impact. The short-term evaluation is a faster and cheaper method, although it may suffer from having an overly narrow focus. The long-term evaluation, while more comprehensive than a short-term evaluation, may require more financial resources than the agency has available.

The question of what should be evaluated, and how, raises the problem of bias, along with potential ethical and political problems. Does the researcher use the yardstick for success employed by the sponsoring agency, or should the evaluator exercise an independent point of view in determining success or failure of the program? For example, consider a program designed to teach high school students the basic fundamentals of comparative food shopping. One way of measuring the success of the program is to evaluate the students' scores on a standardized questionnaire designed to measure retention of the material covered. Although this criterion of success might satisfy school administrators and teachers, there are other criteria that can also be used. One could measure the degree to which the students share the information with their families, to what extent they actually use the information when in the supermarket, and the length of time they retain and use the new information.

It should be evident that the way in which success or failure is measured will involve political decisions. Any social program will appear to be more valuable when measured by certain criteria and not by others. Thus, the researcher may be under strong pressure to use criteria influenced by various interested parties or shaped by his or her own personal values. The best way to avoid an evaluation bias toward the interests of one party is to consult with all interested parties during the planning stages.

Prediction

Sample surveys are most often used to predict the future. Public opinion polls reporting voter preference in an upcoming election are a common example. Other examples might include surveys used to predict future automobile sales, the size of future wheat deals with Russia, or the number of college students who will be enrolled in the year 1985.

Social Indicators

In recent years, surveys have been employed to develop social indicators which, it is hoped, will provide a measure of the social and political feeling in the country comparable to the economic indicators used to measure the state of the economy.

Conclusions

Surveys can be designed with many research objectives in mind. Some of these include:

Exploration of the various factors composing an issue.

Descriptions of the people, events, or phenomena involved with an issue.

Prediction of future trends or events related to an issue.

Development of social indicators.

EXERCISE 3.1: Research Objectives for a Sample Survey

Using your public policy issue as a topic, write out the major research objective(s) you hope to accomplish with your sample survey.

III: TARGET POPULATION

The results of any survey will generalize only to the population from which the sample is drawn. Thus, it is necessary to develop a concise definition of the target population -- that group of subjects about which information is desired. If the study is interested in national opinion about doctors' strikes, it is not enough to study Washington, D.C., Troy, New York, or Pullman, Washington.

In order to begin to define the target population, it is necessary to designate the geographic or physical limits to be included in the survey. For example, is the survey a national one covering all 50 states, a survey of local schools, or a survey of statewide agencies? After the geographic limits have been formulated, the next decision to be made is to establish what population or populations within that area are of interest; that is, what groups of subjects does the surveyor want to be able to generalize about? One survey could examine several different populations using the same set of respondents at the same time. For example, a citywide survey of police precinct stations might consist of a survey of the buildings themselves, the number of jail cells, offices, and committee rooms in each station. A second population might be concerned with the policemen in the one station; how many there are and what they do during an 8-hour shift. A third possible population that might be covered is the officers in each station; how many hours of community relations-type activity they are involved in, how often they patrol the streets. Using the example of the sample survey on food, one population of interest might be heads of households, another teenagers, and a third, the kitchens in each of the homes. In each of these examples, there is some overlap of populations -- for instance, one might be the head of a household and a teenager at the same time. If the survey is directed toward including possible subgroups of a population, then it will be able to make generalizations about each subgroup. A survey designed to cover both heads of households and teenagers who are food consumers would be able to make statements about both teenage heads of households as food consumers and teenagers as food consumers. A survey which has as its target population only heads of households would be able to generalize about teenage heads of housholds as food consumers, but would not be able to make statements concerning teenagers as food consumers, even though some of the heads of households may have been teenagers. The question of pinpointing the survey's target population should be carefully thought out and answered early in the planning stages.

EXERCISE 3.2: Target Population

What is the target population of your sample survey?

____

IV: TYPES OF SAMPLING PROCEDURES

Underlying the well-run sample survey is the concept of the sample. A sample is that portion of the target population which has been selected to represent the target population. Sampling is the operational procedure used to select that sample. This section will introduce several forms of random and nonrandom selection procedures.

Random sampling is a procedure in which all subjects have an equal chance of being selected. In nonrandom sampling, subjects are not selected by chance; they do not all have an equal probability of being chosen. The last section deals in part with sample size; i.e., how many subjects should be contacted in order to have a reasonably good-size sample -- one that allows generalizations to be made about the target population with a certain level of confidence. One thing that should be kept in mind is that a sampling procedure is never good or bad in itself -- it must be evaluated by its ability to satisfy the objectives of the survey.

A.   Nonrandom Sampling Procedures

1.   Haphazard Collections

This sampling procedure relies on subjects, informally met or readily available, such as shoppers in a shopping center or students in a classroom. This procedure does not allow the survey designer to generalize beyond the people interviewed but is frequently used when time or money is limited.

2.   Judgment Sampling

With this procedure, the subjects chosen by the interviewers are those felt to be most representative of the target population. A major limitation of this sampling procedure is that interviewers may have different ideas about who would be a typical representative.

3.   Quota Sampling

Using this procedure, subjects are selected for the sample according to their proportion in the target population. If the target population contains 25 percent Catholics, the total number of Catholics included in the survey will ideally also equal 25 percent. The selection of delegates at the 1972 Democratic convention is an example of an attempt at quota sampling using the entire country as a target population. As with judgment sampling, the weakest aspect of this technique is the determination of the individuals to be included in the quota. Different interviewers may hold different views as to who should be contacted, which would add an unknown amount of bias to the results.

4.   Expert Sampling

This type of sampling relies on the opinion of experts as to which subjects are representative of the target population and should be included in the survey. The major limitation of this method is that experts may differ on those subjects to be contacted. This technique can provide interesting case histories, but it is not a dependable source of information for making generalizations on the target population.

5.   Purposive Samples

This method selects subjects from certain subgroups in the target population. The subgroups are chosen because of their bearing on the hypothesis to be tested. Purposive sampling can be of some value if random sampling is used at each stage in the survey design.

B.   Random Sampling

The following sampling procedures rely to a greater or lesser degree on random chance to define which subjects will be contacted. For statistical reasons which are beyond the scope of this chapter, sampling procedures utilizing random chance for subject selection provide the best estimates or generalizations about the target population.

1.   Simple Random Sampling

This method chooses each subject through a random process in which each unselected subject has the same chance of being chosen as any other subject on each draw. The selection of a particular subject could be made on the basis of flipping a coin, tossing a

pair of dice, or most commonly, with some type of random-numbers
generator, usually a random-numbers table or a computer program.
Each subject is given a number, and when that number comes up on
the dice or is found in the random-numbers table, the subject
is included in the survey. This process continues until a
sufficient number of subjects has been selected. Generally, once
a subject has been chosen, that subject is not eligible to be
selected a second time.

Simple random sampling may not be feasible for a number of
reasons. For example, it may not be economically or physically
possible to contact people all over the city or county for a
survey involving a medical procedure such as a chest x-ray with
its complex attendant equipment. Also, a current and complete list
of the subjects in a target population may not be available. For
these and other reasons, researchers have developed successful
variations on simple random sampling which are vastly better than
nonrandom procedures.

2. Stratification Sampling

This is a method that splits the target population into subgroups. Once the subgroups have been determined, the same or
different selection procedures can be used on each of the subgroups.
For example, suppose the researcher wanted to conduct a survey
using 200 subjects. The target population might be working men and
women containing 60 percent union members and 40 percent nonunion
members. Using this method, the researcher would conduct 120 interviews with the subjects randomly chosen among the union members,
and 80 interviews, again with the subjects randomly chosen among
the nonunion members.

3. Cluster Sampling

As the name implies, cluster sampling involves choosing the
subjects to be interviewed in clusters or groups, rather than
singly as done in simple random sampling. Usually, the clusters
are naturally occurring groups within the target population, for
example, the banks, hospitals, or voter precincts in a community.
A random selection is made of these natural clusters and within
each cluster either all the subjects can be interviewed or a
random sample of the subjects can be contacted. This procedure
will most likely produce results that are slightly less accurate
than those from a single random sample. That may be a small price
to pay, however, compared to the increased convenience and reduced
costs of a cluster sample as opposed to a simple random sample.

4. Systematic Selection Sample

This third variation on simple random sampling involves
choosing the subjects from a list of the members of the target

population. The researcher should be certain that the people are
not listed in any symptomatic fashion such as grade point average
or income level, which would introduce an unknown bias into the
results. Following a random start, every nth subject on the list
is included in the sample. For example, let us suppose that the
list of the target population contains 1000 members and the
researcher plans to interview every 10th member. He or she would
look up the starting point in a table of random numbers. If that
number were 37, then the subjects contacted would be numbers 37,
47, 57, and so on, until the end of the list was reached.

C.   Conclusions

There are two basic types of sampling procedures: random
and nonrandom. The nonrandom procedures include haphazard collec-
tions, judgment sampling, quota sampling, expert sampling, and
purposive sampling. While nonrandom samples are valuable in
certain instances, they do not allow one to make statements about
the target population with as much confidence as do random
sampling, stratification sampling, cluster sampling, and systematic
selection sampling. Random sampling gives the most accurate esti-
mation of the true values of the factors being studied in the
target population.

EXERCISE 3.3: Sampling Procedures

Give a detailed account of how your sample will be drawn.

V. INFORMATION-GATHERING TECHNIQUES AND TYPES OF RESPONSES

There are four major methods used to gather information -- the face-to-face interview, the telephone interview, the mail questionnaire, and the self-administered questionnaire given in a group setting such as a club meeting or a classroom. Before writing the questions, the researcher must decide which of these methods will be used.

A. Information-gathering Techniques

There are some important advantages in having information collected by an interviewer, whether face-to-face or over the telephone. First, the interviewer can stimulate the subject's initial interest, which, in turn, increases the probability that the person will take part in the survey. Second, by creating a supportive atmosphere for answering the questions, the interviewer may increase the subject's motivation to respond in a thorough and straightforward fashion. Third, the interviewer has more flexibility in asking questions and can clear up any ambiguities in the subject's response. (With a self-administered question- naire, the subject may skip those questions not fully understood, thereby reducing the accuracy of the survey.) Fourth, using an interviewer to administer the questionnaire reduces the problem which might occur with a self-administered questionnaire due to the literacy/educational level, or visual acuity of the subjects. Finally, the interviewer can control the sequence in which ques- tions are asked which might be important when later questions affect those that come before.

The very advantages inherent in the personal interview can be turned into disadvantages when compared to the self-administered questionnaire. The greatest advantage of the self-administered questionnaire is its relatively low cost and ease of administration in contrast to the face-to-face interview and the telephone survey. An interviewer must be paid a salary, and travel and other expenses involved with being out in the field. He might, moreover, get bored with the survey, become ill, leave town, or find another job, creating the perennial problem of interviewer turnover. Or, personal interviewers themselves may be biased in one direction or another so that presentation of the questionnaire may differ. Finally, a self-administered questionnaire may be advantageous when dealing with very personal or embarrassing issues. The subject may feel more comfortable about answering certain questions on paper, rather than responding to a stranger.

Telephone Interviews

This method has many of the strengths of a face-to-face interview and is substantially cheaper to conduct. In addition, subjects suspicious of a person on their doorstep might be willing to talk to the same person over the telephone. However, the telephone survey also suffers from serious limitations, among which is the difficulty of establishing and maintaining the level of rapport that can be developed with a face-to-face interview. The second problem is that the subject can terminate the interview by simply hanging up the phone. Thus, the questionnaire used in a telephone survey must be short and easy to answer.

Mail Questionnaires

The major advantage of mail surveys is their relatively low cost, while their major limitation is their low response rate. There are three factors which should be kept in mind when developing a mail survey. First, the more work a subject is required to perform, such as answering a long questionnaire or searching for a stamp, the lower the response rate. Second, a personally typed covering letter or the use of first-class mail very likely will increase the response rate. Third, the greater the subject's interest in the outcome of the survey (for example, a survey within a company concerning salary increases), the higher the response rate will be.

B.   Open-ended and Closed Responses

After determining the method of gathering information, the researcher must decide if the survey will contain questions that are open-ended response, closed response, or some combination of the two.

1. Open-ended Responses

Open-ended response questions are those that allow subjects to answer the question in whichever manner they see fit without restrictions imposed by the questionnaire's designer. An example of this type of question is: "There has been a great deal of concern about the rising cost of food. How do you handle the problem of rising food costs?"

The most important advantage of the open-ended response question is that the respondents can answer using their own reasoning and thinking patterns. These answers will often be filled with quotable material to lend color to the final report. In addition, such questions may provide a useful source of information from which to generate hypotheses. Another advantage is that open-ended responses do not produce answers where none exist, which may be a problem with closed-response questions. Finally, this type of question can provide a chance for subjects to "warm up" at the beginning of the interview. The major limitation to this type of response question lies in the difficulty of digesting and making sense out of the answers given. The range of answers may be so varied that it would be difficult to make meaningful comparisons between subjects. Another problem is that interviewers will be variously skilled in recording verbatim responses which, in turn, will bias the results of the survey.

2. Closed Responses

As the name implies, this type of question limits the kinds of answers the subject gives, requiring a choice of one or more of the answers provided by the questionnaire. The following is an example of closed-response questions:

There has been a great deal of concern about the rising cost of food. How do you handle the problem of rising food costs? (Check all that apply.)

______ purchase cheaper types of foods
______ substitute other types of food in your daily diet
______ purchase large amounts of an item which is on sale
______ eat at restaurants less often
______ invite fewer people over to eat a meal at your home
______ don't know

The major advantage of closed-response questions is that the answers given by the subjects are comparable and limited in number. This, in turn, makes coding and analyzing the data much easier. In addition, this type of question requires less skill and effort on the part of the interviewer, and is easier for the subject to answer. The most serious drawback is that the closed-response question may put words in the subject's mouth by supplying answers he may not have thought of by himself. Most subjects do not want to admit that they have not heard of an issue and they can conceal this fact by choosing one of the answers provided. They may also be inclined to select a "don't know" response, thus avoiding the time and energy required to think about the question.

EXERCISE 3.4: Information-gathering Techniques

What method will you use to gather information? Describe any problems or limitations of the technique.

EXERCISE 3.5: Type of Response

Will you use open or closed responses? Why? Give a sample survey.

C.   <u>Bias in the Sample Survey</u>

A survey is rarely as neat and concise as one would like. Its design and application are not influenced solely by the scientific method. The survey is a product of people operating in the area of the real world and therefore is susceptible to the influences of many actors. Bias is any type of systematic error in the data collected by a sample survey leading to a difference between the sample value and the true population value. The problem of bias is constant in a sample survey. A possible source of bias is the agency or group supporting the survey. It may have a vested interest in seeing that the results of the survey are in accordance with its own position on an issue, since a great deal of money or political influence may be riding on the outcome of the survey. The funding agency may want to decide which problem is of interest and designate the type of relevant information collected to the exclusion of other kinds of information. While it is natural that the sponsoring agency assist in formulating the sample survey objectives, the researcher should be aware of the potential biases of the agency and strive to minimize their impact. The day-to-day working relationship between the researcher and the sponsoring agency will influence all aspects of the sample survey. That influence may introduce biases not only in the formulation of the problems to be studied, but also in the hypotheses to be tested, the selection of the respondents, the wording of the questions, the analysis of the information collected, the explanation of the final outcome, and the utilization of the results. While it is not being suggested that every agency is trying to blatantly pressure the researcher to produce favorable results, the researcher should always make an effort to reduce potential bias regardless of the source.

Another source of bias lies in the answers given by the respondents who may report the answers they believe the researcher wants to hear, rather than their true opinions. The respondent may give only socially desirable answers, i.e., those which put him in compliance with society's mores and values.

<u>Minimizing Bias</u>

At the very least, the researcher should employ intellectual honesty and openness as the first step against bias in sample surveys. In addition, several other precautions can be taken to counteract bias. At each stage, the research design should be reviewed by a range of interested parties. These reviewers could indicate, for example, whether they thought the survey was prejudiced toward some group or whether the initial description of the results contained ideological overtones. If opposing groups agree that the survey is impartial and will generate objective data, the

researcher can be fairly certain that the survey will not suffer
ideological bias.

A second precaution is to seek outside expert opinion about
the appropriateness of the sample design. An expert can determine if the instructions for deciding who will be contacted to
answer the survey follow the laws of probability sampling.

Finally, the questionnaire to be used in the survey should
be reviewed by a panel of experts to determine the objectivity
of the items being used. Leaders of the interested groups could
also criticize the questionnaire items for potential sources of
bias.

EXERCISE 3.6:   Bias and Other Problems

Do you foresee any bias in your sample survey? If so, from
where? Do you foresee any other problems such as excessive cost
or nonresponse? Please explain.

CHAPTER FOUR: DESCRIPTIVE STATISTICS FOR PUBLIC POLICY ANALYSIS

THE PRIMARY OBJECTIVE:

To introduce you to basic statistical skills used in the analysis of public policy issues.

UPON COMPLETION OF THIS CHAPTER, YOU WILL BE ABLE TO:

* Arrange small data sets into tabular form.

* Organize large data sets into frequency distributions.

* Construct and interpret graphic displays of data.

* Calculate and distinguish among several basic statistics.

* Perform data analysis and interpretation using these statistics.

(Based on PS-20: Descriptive Statistics for Public Policy Analysis. Gary Hammerstrom and Amy M. Kafton, Croton-on-Hudson, NY: Policy Studies Associates, 1979.)

I: PRESENTATION OF STATISTICAL DATA

Objectives

- To arrange data sets into tabular form expressed in units relevant to your audience.

- To learn the importance of proper data documentation.

- To learn the appropriate statistics for data scaled at different levels of measurement.

A. Tabular Methods

Data are often presented in a textual form that is both uninteresting and unenlightening. For example:

> According to the National Safety Council, motor vehicle travel in the United States has increased from 420 billion miles in 1950, to 600 billion miles in 1955, 720 billion miles in 1960, 900 billion miles in 1965, and 1100 billion miles in 1970.

However, the same data are much easier to read if arranged in tabular form such as in Table 4.1.

From this table, it is easy to see the dramatic change in the variable (a characteristic which may take on different values) over the time series (the pattern of a series of values arranged in a time sequence).

Tabular methods are a widely accepted means of organizing small sets of data for rapid visualization and understanding. A table requires:

- A title which clearly explains its nature.

- Data elements carefully listed under headings which clearly specify the units of measure.

- Documentation of the data source.

TABLE 4.1: Motor Vehicle Travel in the U.S.

Year	Vehicle Travel (billions of miles)
1950	420
1955	600
1960	720
1965	900
1970	1,100

Source: <u>Accident Facts</u>, Chicago: National Safety Council, 1974, p. 22.

In presenting statistical data, the researcher must consider the relevance of units of measure to the audience which will be using the data. Examine Table 4.2. Although this table shows the growth in Japan's economy, the total magnitude of the economy is not evident to American readers. Do you know the exchange rate between U.S. dollars and Japanese yen? Most people reading Table 4.2 will not know either. Thus, it is important to express this data in terms that are most easily understood by the intended audience. Table 4.3 presents the same information, but converted to U.S. dollars.

Table 4.3 makes more sense to an audience which has a better perception of the value of the dollar than it does of the yen. But we are still dealing with very large quantities. How impressive is a gross national product of $294.1 billion? Most social scientists, including students, probably have an idea of the current U.S. gross national product, but few can remember what it was 10 or 20 years ago. Thus, to give a more complete description of the size and expansion of Japan's gross national product, data should be expressed in U.S. dollars and a comparison made with U.S. gross national product data as in Table 4.4.

In choosing units of measure it is thus important to consider the magnitude of the measurement. What may be a totally understandable unit at one level of magnitude may be difficult to grasp at another. For example, most everyone can visualize the approximate size of 1 square mile. Yet, should you report that 6200 square

TABLE 4.2: Gross National Product of Japan,
1950-1970 in Five-Year Intervals

Year	G.N.P. (billions of yen)
1950	11,310.3
1955	17,576.1
1960	27,266.9
1965	44,258.9
1970	78,083.5

Source: _1976 World Book Atlas_, Washington, D.C.: The World
Book, 1976, p. 16.

TABLE 4.3: Gross National Product of Japan,
1950-1970 in Five-Year Intervals

Year	G.N.P. (billions of dollars)
1950	$ 42.6
1955	66.2
1960	102.7
1965	166.7
1970	294.1

Source: _1976 World Book Atlas_, Washington, D.C.: The World
Book, 1976, p. 16.

TABLE 4.4: Gross National Product of Japan and the
U.S., 1950-1970 in Five-Year Intervals

Year	G.N.P. JAPAN (billions of dollars)	G.N.P. U.S.
1950	$ 42.6	$ 519.1
1955	66.2	639.9
1960	102.7	712.5
1965	166.7	902.6
1970	294.1	1,055.6

Source: __1976 World Book Atlas__, Washington, D.C.: The World
Book, 1976, pp. 16, 20.

miles of the U.S. have been stripmined since 1945, you might have
trouble communicating a perception of area to your readers. Were
you to add a meaningful size comparison such as that 6,200 square
miles is approximately the size of Massachusetts, Connecticut, and
Rhode Island combined, then the statistic would be much easier to
comprehend.

Thus, in considering units of measure, keep the following
points in mind:

. The units of measure should be relevant to or commonly
  understood by your target audience.

. The magnitude of measurement should be easily compre-
  hensible to your target audience. If in doubt, provide some basis for comparison.

B. Data Documentation

To document data simply means to cite the source from which
the data were obtained or derived. Data sources can be cited by

using standard footnoting and bibliographic techniques, with the footnotes placed at the bottom of the appropriate page or collected at the back of the work. With data displays such as graphs or tables (such as Tables 4.1 and 4.2), you should include the data citation in the display.

However presented, the citation should conform to standard literary style guides. When using data which is not your own, be as careful as possible that it is accurate and then cite it completely. You must provide adequate information so as to allow the readers the opportunity to consult the original sources of data if they desire further information.

Proper data documentation is not only a matter of honesty (to knowingly omit credit is plagerism), but also a matter of scholarly expedience. If data which you have used and cited are later found to be in error, you will not have to bear the responsibility for those errors, and although your conclusions may consequently be invalid, it will be for reasons beyond your control.

C.   Levels of Measurement

A knowledge of the type of measurement and scale used in developing data is quite important to the selection and interpretation of statistics. Certain statistics are usable only with specific appropriate scales. There are four major types of scales of measurement, classified in terms of their mathematical properties.

1. Nominal Scales

This type of measurement deals with qualitative variables and categorization. Qualitative variables differ in kind rather than amount. You can say whether observations are the same or different, but not whether one has more or less of the quality in question. For example, Republican and Democrat are two categories of political affiliation. They are different, but a Democrat does not represent any more of the variable "political affiliation" than a Republican. Nominal scales do not rank qualitative categories; they simply record the frequency of occurrences in each category, and speak in terms of similarities or differences. Categories may be designated by numbers, but these merely serve as labels or substitutes for names. For example, airlines use numbers to identify their flights, but that does not mean, say, that traveling on flights #100 and #300 will get you to the same location as taking flight #400. Similarly, we do not expect football player number 14 to play twice as well (or necessarily better ball) than player number 7. Flight schedules and football rosters are both nominal scales.

2. Ordinal Scales

In this system of measurement, qualitative variables are used also, but they are ordered by ranking. Not only do we note whether A is different from B, but whether A is greater than or less than B. This is a measure of differences in position between elements along some specified continuum, but with no indication of the magnitude of the differences. For example, the order of finish in a beauty contest is an ordinal scale -- although the judges decide that one contestant is prettier than another, we cannot assume that the second runner-up is twice as pretty as the fourth runner-up.

Other examples of ordinal scales include social class (upper, middle, lower), rank ordering of political candidates according to their popularity in the polls, and rank ordering of occupations according to their prestige. The ordinal scale also serves the functions of the nominal scale by identifying equality and inequality. (Each subsequent scale in our discussion will include all of the functions of the lower-level scales plus new functions and levels of sophistication.)

3. Interval Scales

Interval scales represent quantitative variables which indicate the amount of a characteristic something has. Addition and subtraction can be performed on quantitative variables. Some standard physical unit of measurement is necessary for interval-level scaling so that the distance or interval between any two elements in the scale is the same as the distance between any other two elements. Therefore, the difference between 4 feet and 2 feet is the same as the distance between 501 and 499 feet. Temperature, as recorded in degrees Fahrenheit or Celsius (centigrade), is of interval-level measurement. A temperature rise from 20° to 30° is equivalent to a rise from 80° to 90° in that both changes increase the temperature by 10°.

An additional feature of interval scales is that they do not contain an absolute zero. They may have a zero value which has been arbitrarily assigned, but their absolute zero point is either unknown or meaningless. For example, temperature scales measure the amount of heat present. Yet, the zero point on either the Fahrenheit or Celsius scale does not identify the absence of heat. Thus, in terms of the amount of heat present, 100°F is not twice as warm as 50°F or ten times as warm as 10°F. Also, the year 2000 A.D. does not mean twice as old as 1000 A.D. since the world was not created at the arbitrary 0 A.D. Interval scales do not provide information about the equality of ratios between points on the scale which cannot be done without the existence of an absolute zero.

Note that quantitative variables are continuous -- they are theoretically infinitely divisible; i.e., between any two numbers there can be another. An infant growing from a height of inches to a height of a few feet passes through an infinite number of heights. In contrast, a discrete variable can have only certain values and none in between. For example, the number of people who took an exam might be 35 or 36, but no value between these two figures is possible. A constant is a characteristic which can only have one value -- the number of days in a week is a constant.

4. Ratio Scales

Quantitative variables associated with ratio scales can be added, subtracted, multiplied, and divided. This is possible because such scales have an absolute zero point which indicates the absence of the variable in question and allows for an evaluation of ratios between intervals. Ratio scales include height, weight, speed, population, distance, the number of votes a candidate receives, and the amount of money allocated to a budget. Temperature can also be measured on a ratio scale called the Kelvin scale, which has an absolute zero indicating the complete absence of heat. That point has been determined as equal to $-459.4°F$ or $-273°C$. Although the absolute zero point is known for the Fahrenheit and Celsius scales, they are nevertheless interval scales because their zero point has been arbitrarily placed else-where. Only on the Kelvin scale can we say that $400°$ is twice as warm as $200°$.

Apart from the difference in the nature of the zero point, interval and ratio scales have the same properties and will be treated alike throughout this package.

We have identified four types of scales and measurements and four important scale properties. Table 4.5 summarizes that information.

As statistical techniques are introduced, we will indicate which are most appropriate for data scaled at different levels of measurement.

TABLE 4.5: Properties of Measurement Scales

Scale	Identity and Equality	Order	Equality of Interval	Equality of Ratio
Nominal	Yes			
Ordinal	Yes	Yes		
Interval	Yes	Yes	Yes	
Ratio	Yes	Yes	Yes	Yes

EXERCISE 4.1: Tabular Methods

Choose an article from the <u>New York Times</u> which concerns
a public policy issue. Using at least one real statistic (the
rest can be hypothetical), construct a table. Be sure to properly
label the table and to note the source of the information. Make
a meaningful interpretation by using the table to support a point
about the public policy issue.

II: GRAPHIC METHODS OF DATA DISPLAY

Objectives

. To learn basic graphing skills.

. To construct a variety of graphs appropriate to both direct data tabulations and frequency distributions.

. To interpret a variety of graphic forms according to the nature of the variable relationship presented.

A.   Basic Graphing Skills

A _graph_ is a pictorial representation of data constructed for the purpose of studying changes in variables or for comparing several similar or related variables. The construction and interpretation of a well-drawn graph are not difficult. A graph shows a series of points, each of which defines values to be read on two different scales. These scales express the range of two variables. The horizontal scale is called the abscissa or x-axis, while the vertical scale is called the ordinate, or y-axis. Generally, data such as scores, time, nominal categories, and variables that cause change in other variables are plotted on the x-axis.

To illustrate, we will present the data in Table 4.6 in a graphic form.

We wish to show on the graph that in 1950 the auto insurance premium rate was $69.63. This is represented by a point on the graph defined by the intersection of a line drawn vertically from the value "1950" on the time scale, and a line drawn horizontally from the approximate value "$69.63" on the premium scale.

The dotted lines on the graph represent mental reference lines which would not normally be shown. The remaining pairs of values can be plotted in a similar fashion to yield a graph of five points which can then be connected as in Figure 4.1 to form a broken line graph.

TABLE 4.6: New York State Automobile
Insurance Premium Rates, 1950–1970

Year	Premium Rate
1950	$ 69.63
1955	86.98
1960	108.67
1965	112.87
1970	135.60

Source: "Trends in Insurance Premiums," New York: New York State
Insurance Council, 1972, p. 87.

Figure 4.1: Basic Graphic Format

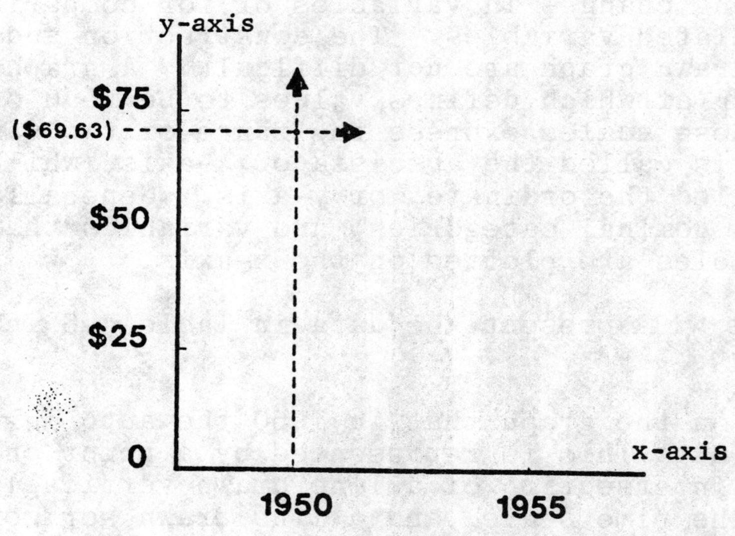

Auto Insurance Premiums in N.Y. State
Source: "Trends in Insurance Premiums," New York:
New York State Insurance Council, 1972, p. 87.

When constructing a graph, remember:

- A graph should always have an explanatory title.
- Axes should be labeled.
- Scales must be calibrated accurately.
- The source of the data must be cited.

It is a good idea to start the y-axis at 0 and, although the size of scale units is optional (e.g., 0, 5, 10 or 0, 10, 20, etc.), consistency is important. The "three-quarter high rule," agreed upon by many statisticians for graphic displays of frequency distributions, states that the y-axis should be about three-quarters of the length of the x-axis. Adherence to these conventions can help avoid biasing of the data presentation.

B. Types of Graphs

1. Bar Graphs

The bar graph makes data comparisons by the use of parallel bars placed either vertically or horizontally on the graph. Figure 4.2 is an example of a vertical bar graph.

Figure 4.2: Vertical Bar Graph

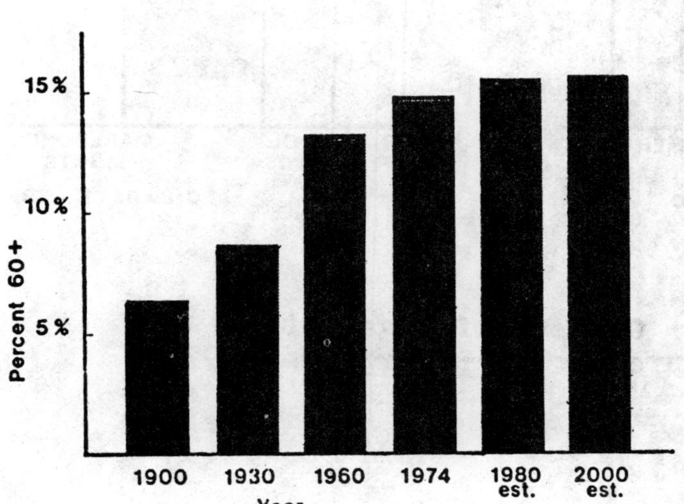

Percent of U.S. Population Age 60+
Source: U.S. Congress, Senate Special Committee on Aging. Nursing Home Care in the U.S., 1974.

In the construction of a bar graph, the length of the bars and the space between them should be consistent and also allow for clear visualization. Bar graphs are useful for representing frequencies or levels of observation in different categories of nominal data, ordinal data, and interval data grouped in frequency categories.

By lengthening or shortening axes, exaggerations or minimizations of differences are possible. Figure 4.3A emphasizes the differences in tar content for three brands of cigarettes. Figure 4.3B uses the same information and gives a different impression by stretching out the x-axis and using different units on the y-axis.

Figure 4.3: Bar Graph Variations

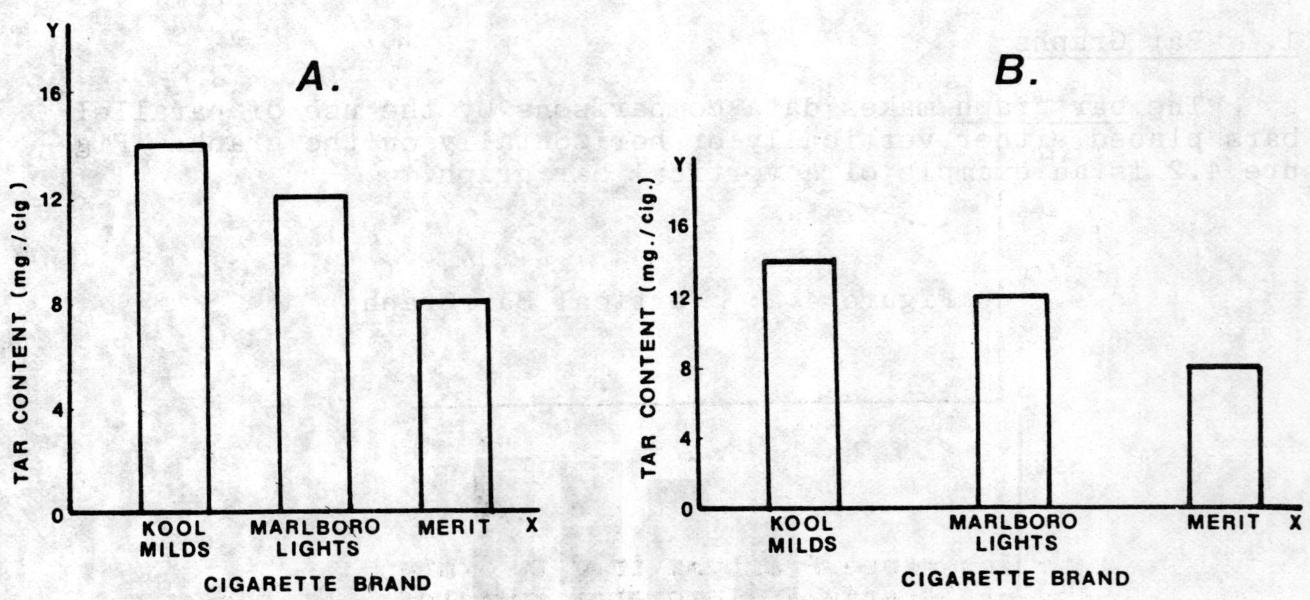

Tar Content of Cigarettes
Source: FTC Report, May 1978.

2. Trend Line

A trend line graph is what most people visualize when they hear
the term "graph." The trend line is derived by plotting time, in
years, months, or days on the x-axis, and something which is changing over time on the y-axis. This type of graph shows the progress
of that which is on the y-axis over time. The trend can also be
projected into the future. This type of display is useful in
monitoring and forecasting. Figure 4.4 is an example of a trend
line.

Figure 4.4: Trend Line

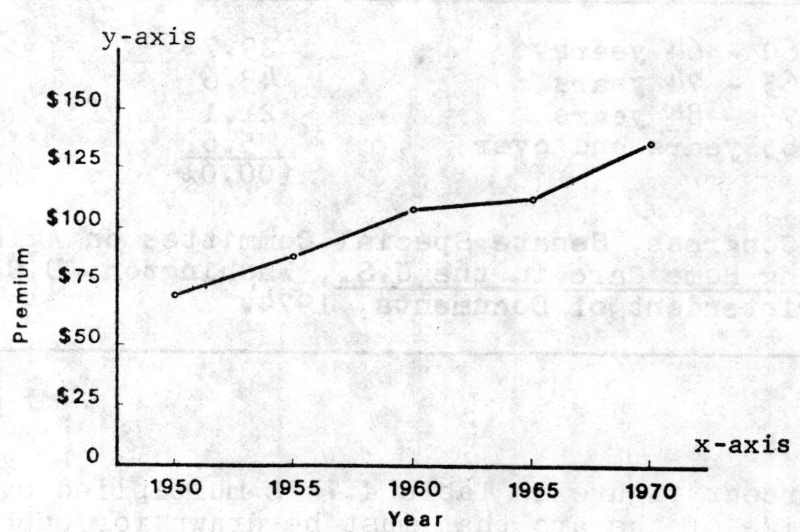

Auto Insurance Premiums in N.Y. State
Source: "Trends in Insurance Premiums, New York:
New York State Insurance Council, 1972,
p. 87.

3. Pie Diagram

The last graphic technique to be described is the _pie diagram_
which is used to show how the component parts of a sum are divided.
The apportionment of government spending or the ethnic composition
of a political party are both examples of subjects amenable to this

technique. A pie diagram is not difficult to construct if you remember that the total of 100% is described by a circle of 360°. Thus, each percentage is equal to an arc of 3.6°. To illustrate, we will construct a pie diagram to show the distribution of people over 60 years of age by age group. The raw data are contained in Table 4.7.

TABLE 4.7: Age Distribution of Population Over 60 in 1974

Age Group	Percent
60 - 64 years	29.7%
65 - 74 years	43.6
75 - 84 years	21.1
85 years and over	5.6
	100.0%

Source: U.S. Congress, Senate Special Committee on Aging, _Nursing Home Care in the U.S._, Washington, D.C.: Superintendent of Documents, 1974.

If each percent figure in Table 4.7 is multiplied by 3.6°, we will know the size of the arc that must be drawn for each segment of the pie.

$$29.7 \times 3.6 = 106.92°$$
$$43.6 \times 3.6 = 156.96°$$
$$21.1 \times 3.6 = 75.96°$$
$$5.6 \times 3.6 = 20.16°$$
$$360.00°$$

A protractor should be used to measure the necessary angles on the circle. It is a good idea to plan ahead so that you have your narrowest angles at the sides where they will be the easiest to label. The labels can either go inside or outside the circle (the latter treatment is preferable if there are especially narrow angles).

    As illustrated in Figure 4.5, the pie diagram can be a very
effective technique for the visual display of data. However, some
caution should be observed. Pie diagrams containing more than
eight segments, or containing several segments with very small arcs
(less than 5°), are difficult to label and often appear so cluttered
as to be difficult to interpret. A pie diagram (or any graph) which
is difficult to interpret or confusing is of no assistance in analyzing data or in presenting the results of analysis.

Figure 4.5: Pie Diagram

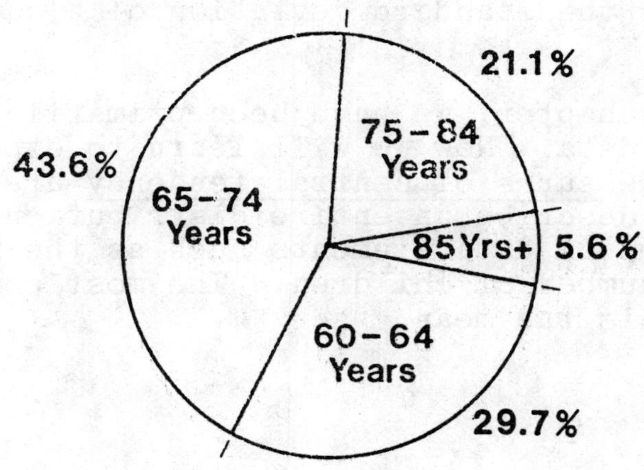

DISTRIBUTION OF U.S. POPULATION AGE 60+

Source: U.S. Congress, Senate Special Committee
          on Aging, Nursing Home Care in the U.S.,
          Washington, D.C.: Superintendent of
          Documents, 1974.

EXERCISE 4.2: Bar Graphs, Trend Lines, and Pie Charts

    Using a recent New York Times article on a public policy issue,
construct a bar graph, a trend line, and a pie chart. At least one
statistic in each display must be real; make a meaningful interpretation by using each display to make a point about the public
policy issue(s).

III: MEAN AND STANDARD DEVIATION

Objectives

. To calculate the mean of a data set.

. To calculate the standard deviation of a data set.

So far in this chapter, we have been primarily concerned with the organization of data. Now we will learn to express our results more efficiently. Measures of central tendency are single, quantitative values which describe an entire distribution in terms of some central location of data elements such as the average person, score, salary, and number of children. The most common measure of central tendency is the mean.

A. The Mean

The arithmetic mean is calculated by summing the values of all the observations in a data set and dividing this number by the total number of observations. Mathematically, the mean can be expressed as:

$$\overline{X} = \frac{X_1 + X_2 + X_3 + \ldots + X_n}{n}$$

where: $\overline{X}$ = the mean,

   n = the number of elements in the data set,

   X_1, X_2, X_3 = the first, second, and third elements, and

   X_n = the last element in the data set

This formula can be written in simpler form using what is called
the summation notation:

$$\bar{X} = \frac{\sum\limits_{i=1}^{n} X_i}{n}$$

where:

$\bar{X}$ = the mean,

n = the number of elements in the data set,

$\sum$ = the Greek letter sigma which is used to mean "the sum of,"

i = the subscript of data element X, and

X_i = each data element

This would be read in the following manner: "The mean of X is equal
to the sum of all X's, within the limits l equals l to l equals n,
divided by n." In other words, add up all the values of X from the
first to the last and divide by the total number of X's.

For example, suppose we wish to calculate the mean of New York
State's automobile insurance premiums from 1950 to 1970 using the
data in Table 4.6:

$$\bar{X} = \frac{69.63 + 86.98 + 108.67 + 112.87 + 135.60}{5}$$

$$\bar{X} = \frac{513.75}{5}$$

$$\bar{X} = \$102.75$$

The mean is an appropriate measure of central tendency only for
interval or ratio level data.

B.   <u>The Standard Deviation</u>

The standard deviation is the most widely used measure of dispersion. The larger its value, the more widely dispersed is the distribution of data. It is usually greater than zero and cannot take a negative value. Also, it is a relative measure of variability. That is, it must be compared to another standard deviation, for a data set of nearly identical mean, to tell us anything really meaningful about data dispersion.

The standard deviation is calculated by using the following formula:

$$Sd_x = \sqrt{\frac{\sum_{i=1}^{n} (X_i - \overline{X})^2}{n}}$$

where:

Sd_x = the standard deviation.

Like the mean, the standard deviation has mathematical properties which make it useful for higher statistical operations and it is therefore often the most desirable measure of dispersion. Again, extreme scores may cause a problem, as they are given more weight when squared. However, for most large data sets, the mean and standard deviation are the appropriate statistics to use.

The size of the standard deviation represents the extent of the variability of individual observations around the mean.

As an example, use the following college quiz scores to calculate the standard deviation:

24	19	17	15	13
23	19	17	15	13
21	19	17	15	12
20	18	16	15	12
20	18	16	14	11
20	17	16	13	11

It is helpful to construct a table in which the mean differences can be calculated, squared, and summed.

TABLE 4.8: Calculations for Standard Deviation

1 Test Score (X)	2 $X - \bar{X}$	3 $(X - \bar{X})^2$
24	7.47	55.80
23	6.47	41.86
21	4.47	19.98
20	3.47	12.04
20	3.47	12.04
20	3.47	12.04
19	2.47	6.10
19	2.47	6.10
19	2.47	6.10
18	1.47	2.16
18	1.47	2.16
17	.47	.22
17	.47	.22
17	.47	.22
17	.47	.22
16	.53	.28
16	.53	.28
16	.53	.28
15	1.53	2.34
15	1.53	2.34
15	1.53	2.34
15	1.53	2.34
14	2.53	6.40
13	3.53	12.46
13	3.53	12.46
13	3.53	12.46
12	4.53	20.52
12	4.53	20.52
11	5.53	30.58
11	5.53	30.58
	82.00	333.44

Standard Deviation: $Sd_x = \sqrt{\dfrac{333.44}{30}} = 3.33$

EXERCISE 4.3: Mean and Standard Deviation

Find a <u>New York Times</u> article on a public policy issue. Calculate the mean and standard deviation using at least one real statistic. Interpret the mean and standard deviation to make a point about the public policy issue.

IV: MEASURES OF ASSOCIATION -- NOMINAL DATA

Objectives

. To develop and apply a contingency table -- a visual
  display of association appropriate to nominal data.

. To calculate a statistic of association, known as
  Yule's Q, which is appropriate to nominal data.

So far we have been concerned primarily with univariate
analysis, or techniques for describing, visually and statistically,
single variables. The final parts of this chapter focus on the
relationship between variables; that is, measures of association
in what is known as bivariate analysis. These measures, known as
correlation coefficients, indicate the degree of association or
correlation between variables which are of nominal, ordinal, interval, or ratio level of measurement. Correlation does not tell us
about causality, but it does indicate the covariation, or direction
and extent of change that occurs in each variable when the other
changes.

The different correlation coefficients have a number of properties in common:

. In a positive or direct relationship, the variables
  change in the same direction; that is, as one increases, the other increases or vice versa.

. In a negative or inverse relationship, the variables
  change in opposite directions; that is, as one increases, the other decreases or vice versa.

. These statistics range from -1.00 to +1.00. Correla-
  tions of +1.00 and -1.00 indicate perfect positive and
  perfect negative realtionships, respectively.

As a general rule, the association is considered strong if the
statistic falls between +.99 and +.60 or -.99 and -.60, moderate if
the correlation is between +.59 and +.30 or between -.59 and -.30,
and weak if the coefficient falls between +.29 and +.001 or between

-.29 and .001. A correlation of .00 indicates no association between variables.

Our study of correlation descriptions and statistics will be limited in the following ways:

. We will consider only propositional relationships, in which the relationship between two empirical variables is defined by indicating the nature of change between the variables and the direction of change. We will not concern ourselves with causation, but only with whether an association of variables exists and the strength of that association.

. We will be concerned only with cases involving two variables -- bivariate analysis. Although many of these techniques are appropriate to multivariate analysis, where more than two variables are considered, this is a more complex subject, and beyond the scope of this package.

A.   Contingency Table

The first correlation coefficients we will explore are used when at least one of the two variables is nominally scaled. They are also well suited for ordinal data and can even be used with interval and ratio data, although there are better measures of association for these types of data.

Let us assume that we are interested in testing the degree of association of sex and political affiliation in a particular community, and propose that "Democratic party registrants are more likely to be women." The determination of these variables can be made from public voter registration data.

What we are looking for is the joint occurrence of two conditions: female sex and Democratic party affiliation. This implies that we might expect another joint occurrence: male sex and Republican party affiliation. In fact, four joint occurrences are possible:

1. Female sex and Democratic party affiliation.
2. Female sex and Republican party affiliation.
3. Male sex and Democratic party affiliation.
4. Male sex and Republican party affiliation.

Our proposition says that we expect outcomes 1 and 4 to be high, and outcomes 2 and 3 to be low.

A means for visually displaying such joint occurrences or outcomes is called the contingency table. The general form of a contingency table is Table 4.9.

TABLE 4.9: Contingency Table

	X	X'	
Y	(a)	(b)	a + b
Y'	(c)	(d)	c + d
	a + c	b + d	n

X and Y = the presence of the propositional conditions,

X' and Y' = the absence of the propositional conditions,

a, b, c, and d = the conditional frequencies which indicate
the number of joint occurrences of XY,
X'Y, XY', and X'Y'.

a + b, c + d,
a + c, and b + d = the marginal frequencies which are the number
of individual occurrences of Y, Y', X, and
X', and

n = the total number of joint occurrences,
a + b + c + d.

Using hypothetical data, we can construct a contingency table
for association between sex and party affiliation.

TABLE 4.10:   Association of Sex and Party Affiliation

	Female	Male	
Democrat	a 157	b 17	174
Republican	c 23	d 136	159
	180	153	333

This table yields a great deal of empirical information about the variables and their degree of association:

1. The sum of the conditional frequencies, or the sum of the vertical or horizontal marginal frequencies, tells us that n, the total number of party affiliations, is 333.

2. The marginal frequencies tell us that of the total there are 174 Democrats and 159 Republicans, and that there are 180 women and 153 men. Thus, there is a slight majority of women and Democrats.

3. The conditional frequencies tell us the number of joint occurrences in each cell. For example, there are 23 females registered as Republicans.

4. It is evident from the distribution of conditional frequencies that our proposition is supported by the data; of the 180 female registered voters, most of them, 157, are Democrats. Conversely, the vast majority of men, 136 out of 153, are Republicans. These data indicate a strong, positive association between women and Democratic party registration.

In contrast, consider the following table in which the marginal frequencies remain the same but the conditional frequencies have changed:

TABLE 4.11:   Association of Sex and Party Affiliation

	Female	Male	
Democrat	91	83	174
Republican	89	70	159
	180	153	333

In this distribution of outcomes, it is difficult to support any proposition regarding association between two variables. Indeed, these data indicate that they are independent of one another.

The contingency table gives us an idea of the association between two variables. It allows us to identify positive associations, in which the a and d cells are dominant, negative associations, in which the b and c cells are dominant, or no association, in which the conditional frequencies are all about equal or are proportional to each other, for example:

50	200
10	40

In constructing a contingency table, use the form shown in Table 4.9 and remember to state the proposition in the title of the table and to cite the source of your data.

B.   Yule's Q

In most cases, it is desirable to obtain a numerical estimate of association. A statistic which will provide this function for nominal data is Yule's Q.* Although Yule's Q has certain limitations, it does provide an approximate measure of association which is preferable to the intuitive impressions available from the contingency table.

Yule's Q is calculated directly from a contingency table as follows:

$$Q = \frac{ad - bc}{ad + bc}$$

where:

$$Q = \text{Yule's Q}$$

a, b, c, and d = the value of the appropriate cell in the contingency table and,

ad and bc = the cell cross-products.

Using Yule's Q, we can calculate estimates of association to verify the conclusions in our sample contingency tables. The calculation for Table 4.10 would be:

$$Q = \frac{ad - bc}{ad + bc} = \frac{(157)(136) - (23)(17)}{(157)(136) + (23)(17)}$$

$$= \frac{21352 - 391}{21352 + 391} = \frac{20961}{21743} = .964$$

This statistic shows that there exists a strong, positive correlation between female sex and Democratic party affiliation, which reaffirms our previous conclusion. The calculations for Table 4.11 would be:

$$Q = \frac{(91)(70) - (89)(83)}{(91)(70) + (89)(83)} = \frac{6370 - 7387}{6370 + 7387}$$

$$= \frac{-1017}{13757} = -.074$$

---

*There are a number of other frequently used statistics which are similar to Yule's Q. These include Chi Square and Gamma. For further information on these statistics, see J.M. Blalock, Jr., Social Statistics, New York: McGraw-Hill, Inc., 1972.

This statistic, being practically zero, indicates that almost no association exists.

Yule's Q is an appropriate estimate of association when you desire a statistic which gives a quick approximation of association and its direction, and your data are arranged in a two-cell by two-cell contingency table.

However, keep in mind that Yule's Q has limitations: since it includes only conditional frequencies and not marginal frequencies, it is regarded as only an approximation, and, if any cell is zero, the statistic cannot be calculated because the result will always be equal to 1.

EXERCISE 4.4: Contingency Table and Yule's Q

Using a recent New York Times article, construct a contingency table and calculate Yule's Q. Use at least one real statistic; the rest can be hypothetical. Make a meaningful interpretation by using the contingency table and Yule's Q to make a point about the public policy issue.

V: MEASURES OF ASSOCIATION -- INTERVAL AND RATIO DATA

Objectives

. To develop and apply the scatterplot, which is a
visual display of association appropriate to interval
and ratio data.

. To differentiate between linear and curvilinear
association.

. To calculate Pearson's r, a statistic of correlation
appropriate to interval and ratio data.

Interval scales, you will recall, contain all the properties
of nominal and ordinal scales, plus information about the absolute
size of the interval between data elements. On this scale, we can
determine not only that one element is larger than another, but
also how much larger. Thus, the mathematical techniques of addition
and subtraction are possible with these scales.

Ratio scales are like interval scales except they contain an
absolute zero point which is lacking in the interval scale. The
addition of this feature means that ratios between intervals become
meaningful. We can now say that one element is twice as large as
another. The mathematical techniques of multiplication and division
are possible with these scales.

The use of these two types of scales allows us to employ still
more sophisticated measures of association, such as the scatterplot,
which is a visual technique for describing data association, and
Pearson's r, a statistic for measuring the degree of correlation
between interval- and ratio-scaled variables.

A.   The Scatterplot

A scatterplot, or diagram is simply a graph in which one variable is scaled along the Y (or vertical) axis and the other is scaled

Figure 4.6: Scatterplots

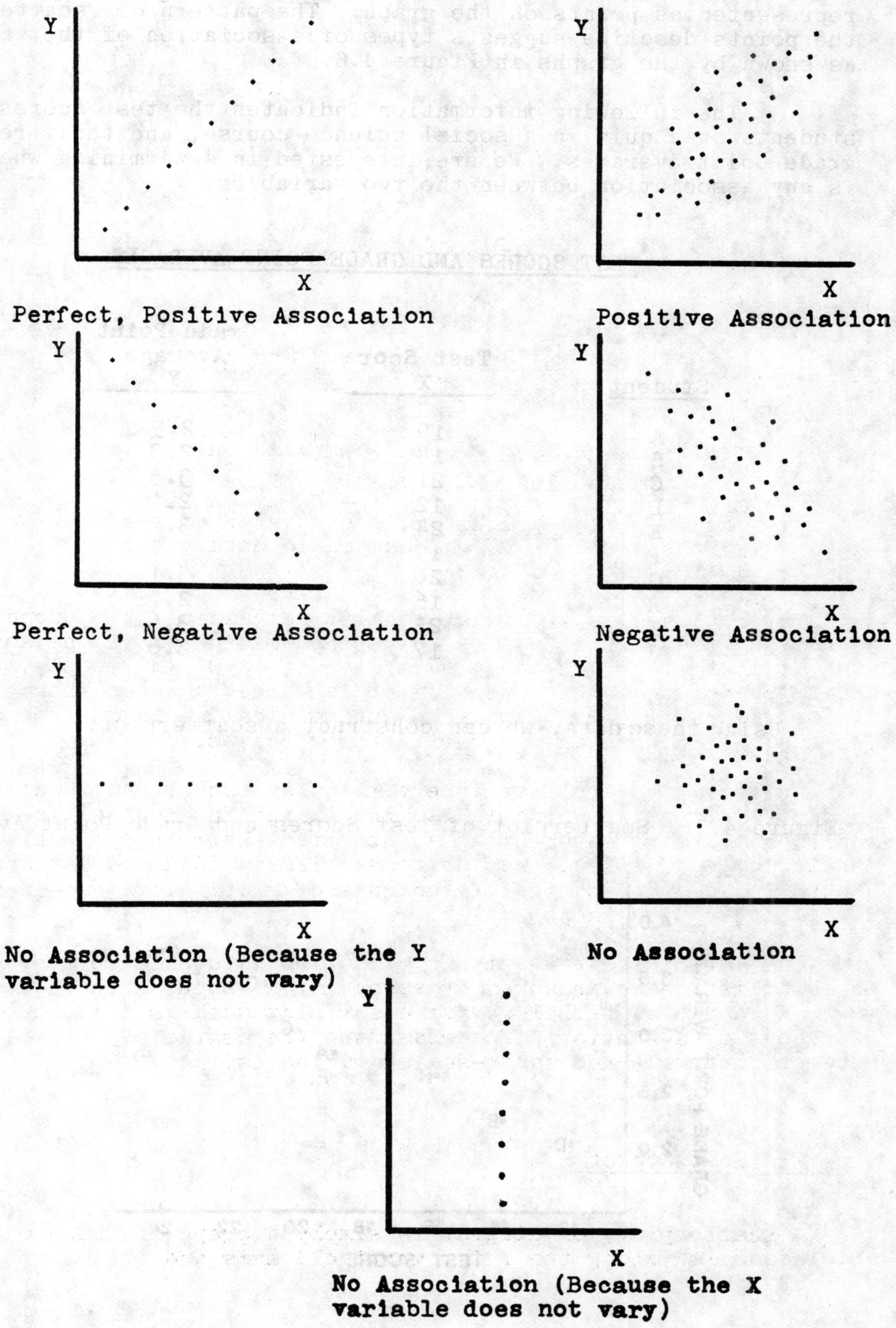
Y
X
Perfect, Positive Association
Y
X
Positive Association
Y
X
Perfect, Negative Association
Y
X
Negative Association
Y
X
No Association (Because the Y variable does not vary)
Y
X
No Association
Y
X
No Association (Because the X variable does not vary)

along the X (or horizontal) axis. Pairs of values can then be
represented as points on the graph. The pattern or "scatter" which
the points describe suggests types of association of the variables,
as shown by the graphs in Figure 4.6.

The following information indicates the test scores of ten
students on a quiz in a social science course, and their respective
grade point averages. We are interested in determining whether there
is any association between the two variables.

<u>TEST SCORES AND GRADE POINT AVERAGES</u>

Student	Test Score X	Grade Point Average Y
A	19	2.9
B	14	2.3
C	21	3.5
D	12	2.1
E	24	3.8
F	19	2.7
G	20	3.1
H	16	2.7
I	23	3.6
J	17	2.6

Using these data, we can construct a scatterplot:

Figure 4.7: Scatterplot of Test Scores and Grade Point Averages

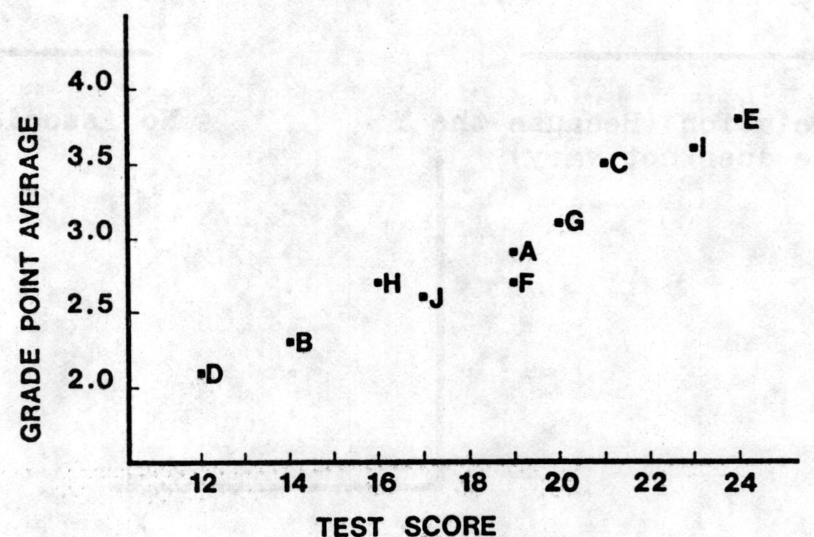

You will note that the points tend to line up from lower left to
upper right. This tells us that "as test score increases, grade
point average increases." We already know that this kind of a
propositional statement defines a positive association.

Thus far, we have graphed only situations in which both variables have been positive. However, it is possible, particularly
in working with ratio scales, to encounter negative values for
variables. Population growth rates can be negative, and government
budget balances and corporate earnings can be negative or deficit,
as spending exceeds revenues. Thus, our graphing techniques must
allow for an expression of these values. Figure 4.8 extends the
X and Y scales into the negative to create a graph which is actually composed of four quadrants. We have only dealt with Quadrant
I thus far. The other three quadrants are defined in terms of their
positive and negative attributes.

Figure 4.8: Signs of X and Y in Four Quadrant Coordinate System

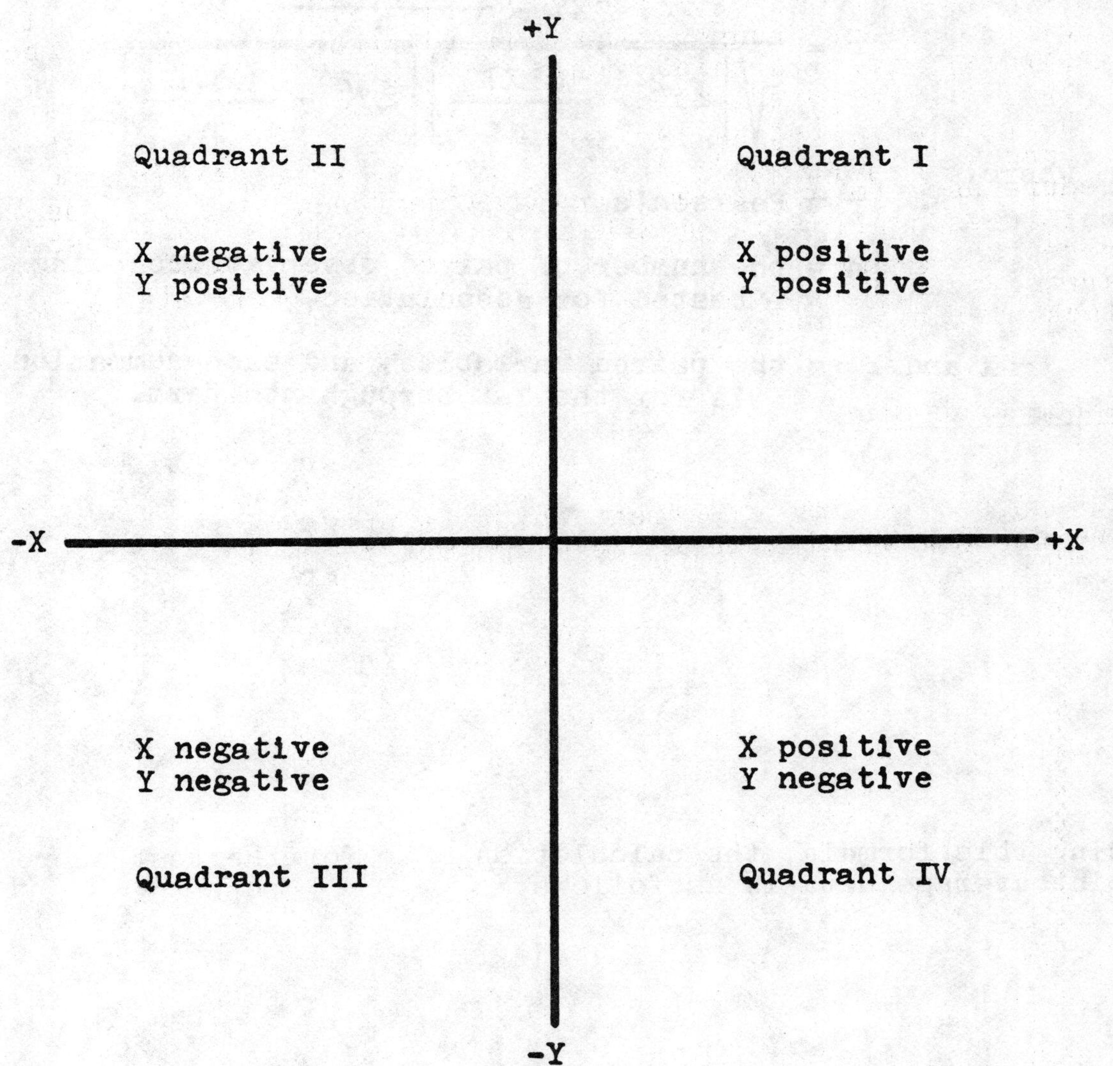

Depending upon the values of the variables, a scatterplot may fall into any of the four quadrants or any combination of quadrants. The conclusions, based on the shape of the scatter, will remain the same regardless of the quadrant involved.

B.   Pearson's r -- The Pearson Product-moment Correlation Coefficient

Pearson's r is a correlation statistic, appropriate to interval and ratio scale data. It varies from -1 to +1 and the interpretation of the scores is the same as with Yule's Q.

It is possible to express Pearson's r in a form which is easy to calculate:

$$r = \frac{\sum XY - \frac{(\sum X)(\sum Y)}{n}}{\sqrt{\left[\sum X^2 - \frac{(\sum X)^2}{n}\right]\left[\sum Y^2 - \frac{(\sum Y)^2}{n}\right]}}$$

where:

r = Pearson's r

n = the number of paired observations being tested for association,

X and Y = the paired variables, and each summation is for the 1st through nth term.

Using this formula, the calculation of r for the test score/grade point average data is as follows:

TABLE 4.12: Worksheet for Pearson's r -- Test Score/GPA Data

X	Y	X^2	Y^2	XY
2.9	19	8.41	361	55.1
2.3	14	5.29	196	32.2
3.5	21	12.25	441	73.5
2.1	12	4.41	144	25.2
3.8	24	14.44	576	91.2
2.7	19	7.29	361	51.3
3.1	20	9.61	400	62.0
2.7	16	7.29	256	43.2
3.6	23	12.96	529	82.8
2.6	17	6.76	289	44.2
$\Sigma X=29.3$	$\Sigma Y=185$	$\Sigma X^2=88.71$	$\Sigma Y^2=3553$	$\Sigma XY=560.7$

$$r = \frac{560.7 - \dfrac{(29.3)(185)}{10}}{\sqrt{\left[88.71 - \dfrac{(29.3)^2}{10}\right]\left[3553 - \dfrac{(185)^2}{10}\right]}}$$

$$= \frac{560.7 - 542.1}{\sqrt{(88.71 - 85.85)(3553 - 3422.5)}}$$

$$= \frac{18.6}{\sqrt{(2.86)(130.5)}}$$

$$= \frac{18.6}{\sqrt{373.23}}$$

$$= \frac{18.6}{19.3}$$

$$= .964$$

There are several factors that may affect the size of Pearson's r:

1. Because Pearson's r is related to the mean, if you have one discrepant pair of observations (e.g., if one observation is high on x and its counterpart is low on y) in a set of data that is otherwise positively linearly related, the calculated correlation will be lower than what is truly representative.

2. Similarly, if the majority of data pairs are negatively linearly related and one pair is positively related, the magnitude of the observed linear relationship will be lowered according to the observed statistic.

3. If the variability of the relationship is too limited, Pearson's r will automatically decrease. For example, in the following diagram the boxed-off area represents extremely homogeneous data which does not usually indicate a high correlation.

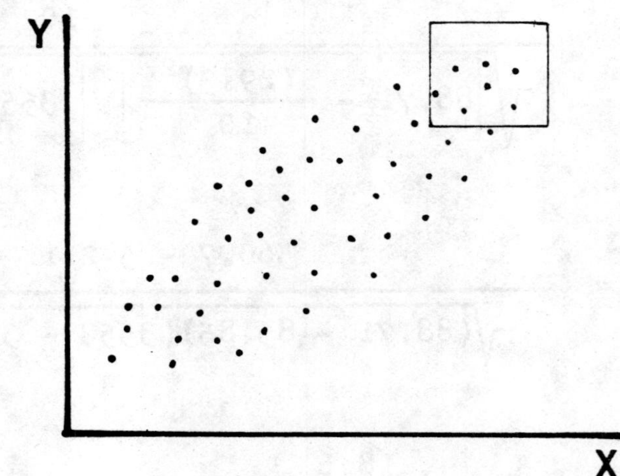

4. If one or both distributions are skewed, the magnitude of the Pearson's r will be reduced unless they are skewed in opposite directions by the same amount. In that case, Pearson's r will increase.

EXERCISE 4.5:   Scatterplot and Pearson's r

Choose a recent <u>New York Times</u> article on a public policy issue. Using at least one real statistic, construct a scatter-plot and calculate Pearson's r. Make a meaningful interpretation by using the display to make a point about the public policy issue.

<u>CHAPTER FIVE: POLICY EVALUATION</u>

THE PRIMARY OBJECTIVE:

This chapter will introduce the student to the concepts and designs used to evaluate social programs.

UPON COMPLETION OF THIS CHAPTER, YOU WILL BE ABLE TO:

* Identify the benefits and costs of a public policy or social program.

* Recognize the need for systematic evaluation of social programs.

* Identify various designs used for the evaluation of social programs.

* Distinguish between poorly designed and well-designed evaluations of social programs.

* Select the most appropriate design, given the social program, available resources, as well as constraints of time, ethical considerations, and potential user's interests.

(Based on <u>PS-11: Designs for Evaluating Social Programs</u>, Lawrence P. Clark, Croton-on-Hudson, NY: Policy Studies Associates, 1976, and a forthcoming learning package by Josephine LaPlante.)

I: AN INTRODUCTION TO THE USE OF BENEFITS AND COSTS OF PUBLIC POLICY

The need for cutting costs at all levels of government has focused much attention on the quantitative techniques which are available to assist decision makers. Benefit-cost analysis is a tool which can help decision makers to evaluate alternatives to determine whether a project should be undertaken and at how large a scale. Benefit-cost analysis need not be a difficult procedure and it is one which is suited to both personal as well as public decision making.

A. Defining Benefits and Costs

Benefit-cost analysis seeks a systematic evaluation of all benefits and costs of a particular project. What is a benefit? What is a cost?

Benefits are anything you gain by undertaking a particular course of action.

Costs are anything you must give up in order to obtain those benefits.

Thus, costs are not only a direct monetary outlay, but should also be thought of as benefits which must be foregone if one alternative is chosen over another. This measurement of costs in terms of benefits which must be sacrificed is what economists call an opportunity cost.

Opportunity costs are inherent in all decisions. When a government decision maker chooses to implement one program rather than another, he is sacrificing the benefits which could have been derived from the next best use of the funds. When implementing a new program requires raising taxes, there is an opportunity cost involved in removing resources from the use of businesses and households. When you make the decision to purchase a record album rather than a book, your opportunity cost equals the benefit you might have derived from reading the book.

Benefit-cost analysis attempts to enumerate all such benefits and costs and then assign values to them. This is where the major problem of benefit-cost analysis arises. How can you determine how much reading a book is worth to you? The answer depends on various factors. If the book is a required text, the opportunity cost of choosing an album over the book might be quite high. On the other hand, the benefits you might derive from a record album could be even higher.

There are several techniques for assigning values to benefits and costs, but they are not without controversy. At this point, the major idea to keep in mind is that all decisions entail costs and benefits and a systematic approach to considering them can greatly improve decision making.

B.   An Informal Application of Some Benefit-Cost Concepts

The decision-making rule of benefit-cost analysis is simply that which common sense dictates:

> A PROJECT SHOULD BE UNDERTAKEN ONLY IF ITS
> BENEFITS ARE AT LEAST EQUAL TO ITS COSTS.

With this rule in mind, let's look at a hypothetical situation and attempt to use benefit-cost analysis to help make a decision.

John, a graduating senior, has been planning to attend graduate school to obtain a Master's degree in Public Administration. He has just been offered a position at a public agency where he has been working as an intern. The position offers a good starting salary and various fringe benefits, including a tuition reimbursement program for coursework related to the job. There is also room for advancement within the agency. However, John believes that he would have been offered a more challenging position if he'd had a Master's degree.

What are the benefits and costs which John should consider? What are the benefits he can hope to obtain by investing a year's time in attending graduate school? What are the costs, including any benefits of the job which he'll have to turn down to attend school?

There are a number of benefits and costs. Let us look at some of them:

Benefits	Costs
Potential higher life-time earnings	Cost of tuition, fees, books
Sense of satisfaction	Loss of earnings from employment
Prestige	Loss of tuition reimbursement
Increased knowledge	Loss of year's worth of experience
Improved job-seeking status	
Benefit to society of better educated citizenry	

The decision is not a simple one.

C. Classifying Benefits and Costs

Some of the benefits and costs outlined in the education example may have seemed more pertinent than others. Some of the more important benefits or costs may have been harder to define. Benefits and costs fall into two categories, direct and indirect, depending on their relation to the particular project being analyzed. Direct and indirect benefits and costs may each be divided into tangible versus intangible effects. Whether an effect is tangible or intangible depends on the nature of the benefit or cost itself. Let's look at these classifications more carefully.

Direct benefits and costs are the primary effects of a given alternative. Indirect benefits and costs are the secondary effects or "side effects" which occur because of a project. Examine the benefits and costs outlined in the education example in this framework:

	Benefits	Costs
DIRECT	Increased earnings	Tuition charges
INDIRECT	Benefit to society	Loss of leisure

Direct and indirect benefits and costs are either tangible or intangible. A tangible effect is one which may be quantified. While tangible effects of projects can be specified in monetary terms, it is often difficult to assign a value which can be generally

agreed upon. In the above breakdown, both the direct benefit of
increased earnings and the direct cost of tuition charges are
tangibles and could be expressed in monetary terms. In a flood-
control project, an indirect tangible benefit might be reduced soil
erosion; an indirect tangible cost might, on the other hand, be
increased soil erosion.

An <u>intangible project effect</u> is a benefit or cost which is non-
monetary in nature. Both the indirect benefit and the indirect cost
noted above, benefit to society, and loss of leisure are intangible
effects. Examples of direct intangible effects might be the same
as those mentioned for indirect, given a different situation where
they would be primary effects rather than secondary. As noted in
the initial breakdown, whether a benefit or cost is direct or indirect depends on its relation to the particular project under consideration. Whether benefits and costs are tangible or intangible
is determined by the nature of the benefit or cost itself.

EXERCISE 5.1: Benefits and Costs

Find a recent news article or editorial which discusses a
particular project or public policy and tell whether the policy is
proposed or existing. Cite a source and give a brief history of
the policy, including where it was proposed, approximate date of
proposal or passage, and the area the policy will affect (local,
state, national). What are the expected costs and benefits of the
policy?

II: THE NEED FOR RESEARCH DESIGN

When a program is implemented, there are certain expected
benefits and costs. The degree to which these benefits are realized
and the costs minimized is a measure of the degree to which the
program succeeds. For example, if a program is designed to provide reliable mass transportation for a small community, and the
transportation is expected to reduce fuel consumption, reduced fuel
consumption is an expected benefit. If fuel consumption is reduced
the program is, to some degree, a success. But if the amount of
fuel saved is very small, and the cost of the mass transit system
very high, the program may be considered a failure. In this case,
the desired benefit was achieved but the costs far outweighed the
benefits.

Unlike a laboratory situation, the policy environment cannot
be isolated. The transportation system could have failed to
improve for many other reasons. Perhaps fuel consumption did not
decrease because although people were using their cars less for
intracity travel, they were using them more for intercity travel.
Perhaps people took more vacations. Perhaps fuel prices fell during
the trial period so that it became cheaper to drive than to take
the mass transportation. All of these factors could have made the
project look like a failure.

Social scientists have developed ways of making observations
systematic so that the number of alternate explanations for the
impact of the program is minimized. With these methods, the expected costs and benefits of the policy can be observed more readily
with minimal interference from other sources. It is these research
designs that will be examined in the remainder of this chapter.

To illustrate why it is not satisfactory to evaluate any
given social program without constructing a systematic plan to
collect and evaluate data, consider the following example.

Suppose that you felt ill on Monday, visited the health
service on Tuesday and received a one-day supply of pills to
alleviate the problem. On Wednesday you feel fine. You are then
asked by the physician whether you feel better. You tell him,
"Yes," truthfully. Assume for simplicity that, in fact, your
health status has improved.

Based on this simple comparison of your condition before receiving the pill versus after, the physician infers tht the pill has "worked," i.e., that the treatment's effects were positive. The size of the effect is gauged from the size of the improvement in health status from the following graph:

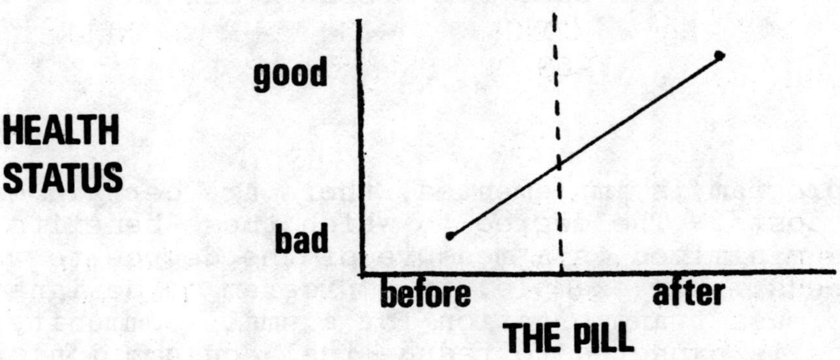

The steeper the slope from A to B, the greater the improvement in health status.

EXERCISE 5.2:   Benefits and Costs in Evaluation

How do your expected benefits and costs relate to the success or failure of your program? What cost or benefit will you study? What is the purpose of your design?

III: SOME BASIC CONCEPTS NECESSARY TO UNDERSTAND TYPES OF RESEARCH DESIGNS

Regardless of design, all attempts at evaluating the impact of a social program consider at least the following seven basic concepts.

1. Dependent Variable

2. Independent Variable

3. Manipulation

4. Confounding Variable

5. Subjects

6. Control

7. Randomization

It is possible that you are familiar with some or all of these concepts. For that reason, you should read only those sections of this part unfamiliar to you.

The material in this part is presented in a glossary format. The concepts are applied throughout the remainder of this chapter, and the purpose here is merely to make sure that you have a general comprehension of what they mean.

A. Definitions

1. Dependent Variable

The dependent variable is the fact which the researcher is interested in explaining. It may be the math ability of high school students, the fluctuations in the oil market, or the effects of compensatory education on preschoolers. In the pill-taking example the dependent variable is the change in your health status. In all cases, the aim is to explain why a variable behaves the way it does.

2. Independent Variable

The independent variable is the variable used to explain the one that is dependent. It is usually thought of as being causally prior to the dependent variable. In the study of compensatory education, the independent variable could be the type of education presented to the preschoolers. In the pill-taking example, the independent variable is the pill.

3. Manipulation

Manipulation occurs when an experimenter can intentionally create variations in the independent variable. These manipulations could be different approaches to teaching preschoolers or the race of the teacher. In the pill-taking example, one manipulation could be the strength of the dosage used in the pill. Another manipulation could be the type of drug used.

4. Confounding Variable

Confounding variables are the rival explanations for the behavior of the dependent variable. The difference in the amount of learning by preschoolers may not be due to different approaches to teaching but to factors outside the classroom such as home environment, number of siblings, etc. In the pill-taking example, the improvement in health may be due to changes in eating habits, more sleep, or any of a host of alternative explanations.

5. Subjects

Subjects are the units upon which the observations are made. They may include the individual preschoolers, nation-states, formal organizations, or government agencies. In the pill-taking example, you are the subject upon which the observations are made.

6. Control

There is within every evaluation either an explicit or implicit comparison: that some collection of subjects is better or worse as a result of the evaluator's treatment or manipulation. The control is that set of data with which the treatment group is compared. The control can be another collection of subjects not receiving the treatment, or it can be a series of measurements taken on the treatment group before it receives the treatment.

7. Randomization

Randomization is the process by which subjects have an equal chance of being assigned to either the treatment group or the control group. The group they end up in is determined purely by chance.

EXERCISE 5.3: Applying the Definitions

State the independent and dependent variables for your design.
The dependent variable should be clearly measurable.

IV: RESEARCH DESIGNS

A. Pre-experimental Designs

The first three designs to be considered are called Pre-experimental Designs. As one can gather from their names, they are not true experiments. Since they are not, they lack the basic power of a true experiment to show what causes what. It is this power which underlies the inferences made by the evaluator about the effectiveness of the social program. To the degree that a research design increases that power, it increases the strength of the inferences derived by the evaluator. The three designs are: One-Shot Case Study, One-Group Pretest/Posttest, and Static-Group Comparison.

In presenting these and the other experimental designs which follow, the code and graphic presentation developed by Campbell and Stanley will be used. An X will refer to the exposure of a group to an experimental treatment or event, the effects of which are to be measured in some fashion. An O represents a process of observaton or measurement. The X's and O's in a given row are applied to the same people or groups. The left-to-right dimension symbolizes the temporal order in which events occur. The X's and O's on top of each other are simultaneous occurrences. The symbol R stands for the random assignment of subjects to separate treatment groups. This randomization occurs at a specific time and is the general procedure used to bring about pretreatment equality of groups. The graphic presentation of parallel rows not separated by dashes represents comparison groups equated by randomization, while those separated by a dashed line are comparison groups not equated due to lack of random assignment.

One-Shot Case Study

In this design, a single group is studied only once after being exposed to some treatment which is presumed to cause a change in the dependent variable. The diagram of such a study is:

$$X \qquad O$$

These studies have such a total lack of control as to be of almost
no value to the evaluator. Fortunately, one almost never sees this
kind of design reported in the literature on program evaluation.
The design is discussed mainly as a minimum starting point. Underlying all program evaluation is the process of comparison, of noting
differences, or of contrasting the changes in the dependent variable.
For such comparisons to be of some value, the things being compared
should be observed with equal care. In this design, a thoroughly
studied single case is implicitly compared with what would have
been had the X not occurred. Studies using this design often collect
copious amount of data on the treatment group in order to buttress
their conclusions. However, these types of studies suffer from
what Campbell and Stanley call the error of 'misplaced precision'
since this potentially vast amount of data in no way compensates for
lack of an explicit comparison with some other group or set of
observations. The One-Shot Case Study is the weakest design to be
considered here and is even less complex than the pill-taking exercise discussed below.

One-Group Pretest/Posttest

This is the design used in the pill-taking exercise. In general, the design looks like this:

$$O_1 \qquad\qquad X \qquad\qquad O_2$$

At O_1, the pretest, you observe that you are not feeling too well.
You go to the health center for the pill treatment, X. One day
later at O_2, the posttest, you notice an improvement in your health
status. For the discussion of this design and the ones that follow,
a small change in the pill-taking example will be made. Assume
that from now on you are part of a larger group of people given the
same drug. This change is done for statistical reasons. The pill-
taking example will be used to illustrate the strengths and weaknesses of this design.

There are several confounding variables which threaten the
internal validity of this design. These confounding variables
offer rival explanations to the hypothesis that X was responsible
for the difference between O_1 and O_2.

One of these uncontrolled confounding variables is history.
Between the pretest observation and the posttest observations, many
other change-inducing events could have taken place besides the
experimental treatment. After a winter of drab and depressing days,
the sun might have come bursting out with all its warmth on the day
that you went down to the health center. Thus, the reason that you
feel better may be due to the beautiful day rather than the pill

you took. In order to be a reasonable rival hypothesis, the event should have occurred to most of the people in the group. History becomes a more credible rival hypothesis for explaining the change, the longer the lapse between the pretest/posttest.

While this design is a weak one, it is an improvement over the One-Shot Case Study.

Static-Group Comparison

Suppose the health center compared the results of your treatment group with another group of students. Such an evaluation design is called a Static-Group Comparison. In this design, a group which was exposed to treatment X is compared to one which was not. This comparison is made to establish the effect of X.

The hope is that the two groups will be equal and thus a valid comparison can be made. Unfortunately, there is no formal way of confirming that the groups would have been equivalent had it not been for the treatment X. This problem, indicated by the dotted line, highlights the major confounding variable not controlled by this design -- selection. If O_1 and O_2 differ, this occurrence might well have happened because different criteria were used to place people in one group or the other. Thus, the groups would have differed even without the experimental treatment. Selection could be a problem in the pill-taking example if the health center put all the sick people in one group and at the time of observation O_2, selected an equal number of healthy students as the comparison group. Since one would not expect all the sick people to be completely cured, the health center might falsely conclude that the drug did not have an effect. In fact, this would not be the case since there is no reason to assume that the two groups were equal had it not been for the taking of the pill.

Pre-experimental Designs: Conclusions

The research designs discussed in this section are the weakest of the designs used in program evaluation since they do a very poor job of controlling rival hypotheses as explanations of the change in the dependent variable. In the next section, three designs which do the best job of controlling rival hypotheses will be considered.

B. <u>True-experimental Designs</u>

Unlike the previous designs, the next three are True-experimental Designs. The basic difference between the three types is the amount of control the evaluator can exercise. Within the context of the design, the evaluator can not only schedule the collection of data, he or she also has some degree of control over the presentation of the independent variables. Through the ability to randomly assign subjects to treatment or control, the evaluator can cut down the number of potentially confounding variables which could be used to cast doubt on his results. The ability to control these factors provides a strong inferential base from which to draw conclusions.

The three designs are: Pretest/Posttest Control Group, Solomon Four-Group, and Posttest-Only Control Group. These three designs, as Campbell and Stanley point out, are those currently recommended in the methodological literature. They are also the most highly recommended designs presented in this chapter for the evaluation of social programs. However, as will be pointed out later, there are some specific limitations in the use of each of these designs which should be taken into consideration. Of the three, the Pretest/Posttest Control is by far the most popular.

<u>Pretest/Posttest Control Group</u>

Suppose the health center, in an attempt to find out the effects of the drug, randomly assigned sick students to one of two groups: an experimental group which will receive the drug, and a control group which will receive no treatment. Assume, for the purpose of illustration, that the health center would take the unethical stand of withholding treatment from patients. Both groups are given a pretest, O_1 and O_3, at the same time. The experimental group then receives the treatment and the control group receives none. After the treatment is completed, both groups are given a posttest, O_2 and O_4, at the same time. The general form of the design is as follows:

$$R \quad O_1 \quad X \quad O_2$$
$$R \quad O_3 \quad \quad O_4$$

History as a confounding variable is controlled since any general events that might have caused an O_1-O_2 difference would have also caused an O_3-O_4 difference. However, you should be aware that this design does not control for unique intrasession history, i.e., a car accident happening in the street outside, a momentary power failure, etc., which occurs while the treatment is being given. The best control method for such problems as the randomization of experimental occasions. The student should try to bring about a balanced representation of such possible sources of error as type of experimenters, time of day, week of the semester, etc.

Using this evaluation design, you would not have to worry about the consequences of a sunny day since both the pill-taking group and the control group would be equally affected.

<u>Solomon Four-Group</u>

Suppose the health center was concerned about the threats to external validity noted in the previous design. It decided to run the Pretest/Posttest Control Group Design again with the addition of two more groups. Now students would be randomly assigned to two other groups, in addition to the two groups from the previous design. One group would be given the treatment and the posttest with no pretest. The other group would be given only the posttest. Again, it will be assumed for purpose of illustration that the health center would withhold treatment from patients. The design would look like this :

$$R \quad O_1 \quad X \quad O_2$$
$$R \quad O_3 \quad \quad O_4$$
$$R \quad \quad X \quad O_5$$
$$R \quad \quad \quad O_6$$

The first two groups replicate the Pretest/Posttest Control Group Design. Thus, this design has the same power to control for alternate explanations as that design. The addition of the two extra groups allows the Solomon Four-Group Design to control for more alternate explanations not controlled for in previous designs. In this way, the generalization of the results is increased. To illustrate, using the pill-taking example, suppose the drug had no effect and the reason you got better was the fact that you were examined by a doctor. If this is the case, then O_2 and O_4 should be greater than O_5 and O_6. If not, then we know it was not the pretest that caused the change in your health status. Now suppose the change is due to an interaction between the pretest and the

drug. For this to be true, O_2 has to be greater than O_5. If that
is not true and you did in fact improve your health status, then
this design provides solid proof for the efficacy of the drug.

Posttest-Only Control Group

There are many situations confronting a program evaluator for
which pretests are inconvenient, likely to be reactive, or inappro-
priate. If that is the case, the Posttest-Only Group Design should
be considered. While it is not likely that a hospital would give a
patient a pill without a prior examination, let us assume for the
moment that this could happen as part of an evaluation program. As
the students came to the health center, they would be randomly
assigned to one of two groups. The first group receives the treatment and a posttest examination. The other group just receives the
posttest examination. The design looks like the following:

$$R \quad X \quad O_1$$

$$R \qquad\quad O_2$$

While the idea of a pretest to determine the comparability of
groups is an old and cherished tradition in research, it is not an
absolute necessity for True-experimental Designs. Within the
limits of a statistical confidence, the explanation of which is
beyond the scope of this chapter, the randomized placement of
subjects into the various groups is a most satisfactory way of
assuring that the groups are initially equal.

Since the two groups are assumed to be initially equal, this
design has the same control over alternate explanations as have
the other two designs in this section.

True-experimental Designs: Conclusions

By far the most popular of the three experimental designs is
the Pretest/Posttest Control Group Design. The Solomon Four-Group
Design is the most comprehensive of the three, but that increase in
comprehensiveness comes at the cost of at least double the effort.
In terms of the actual cost of the evaluation, the Posttest Only
Control Group Design is the cheapest to run.

C.   <u>Quasi-experimental Designs</u>

The next three designs fall somewhere in between the Pre-experimental Designs of Section A and the True-experimental Designs of Section B. There are many natural situations in which the program evaluator, for ethical, political, or practical reasons, cannot randomly assign subjects to groups or control who receives treatment and who does not. However, the evaluator can follow something like an experimental design in the collection of data even though she or he does not have the full control over the independent variables that makes a true experimental design possible. Such collection procedures are called Quasi-experimental Designs. The three designs to be considered are: Time-Series, Nonequivalent Control Group, and Multiple Time-Series.

<u>Time-Series</u>

Since the withholding of treatment is morally wrong, the health center might want to turn to a Quasi-experimental Design to evaluate the efficacy of the drug. Suppose that it measured the individual health status of a group of students over an extended period of time. During that time, students periodically reported to the health center for an examination. At some point in this series of examinations, the health center gave the drug to the students. The design would look like the following:

$$O_1 \quad O_2 \quad O_3 \quad O_4 X O_5 \quad O_6 \quad O_7 \quad O_8$$

Basically, the Time-Series Design contains a series of observations or measurements on a group or individual and the presentation of a treatment manipulation into this time series. The results of treatment are indicated by a discontinuity in the observations made during the time series.

Figure 5.1 represents some of the likely results for a time-series design into which a treatment, X, has been presented to the subjects. It appears from Figure 5.1 that the treatment had some impact in the case of A and B and, conceivably, in the case of C, D, and E. It would not appear that the treatment had any impact in the case of F, G, and H.

The most obvious weakness of this design is the problem of history. There may be some event external to the treatment session that caused the change in the dependent variable. To the degree that you can reasonably discount such outside events as causing

Figure 5.1: Potential Impact of Treatment on Time-Series Data*

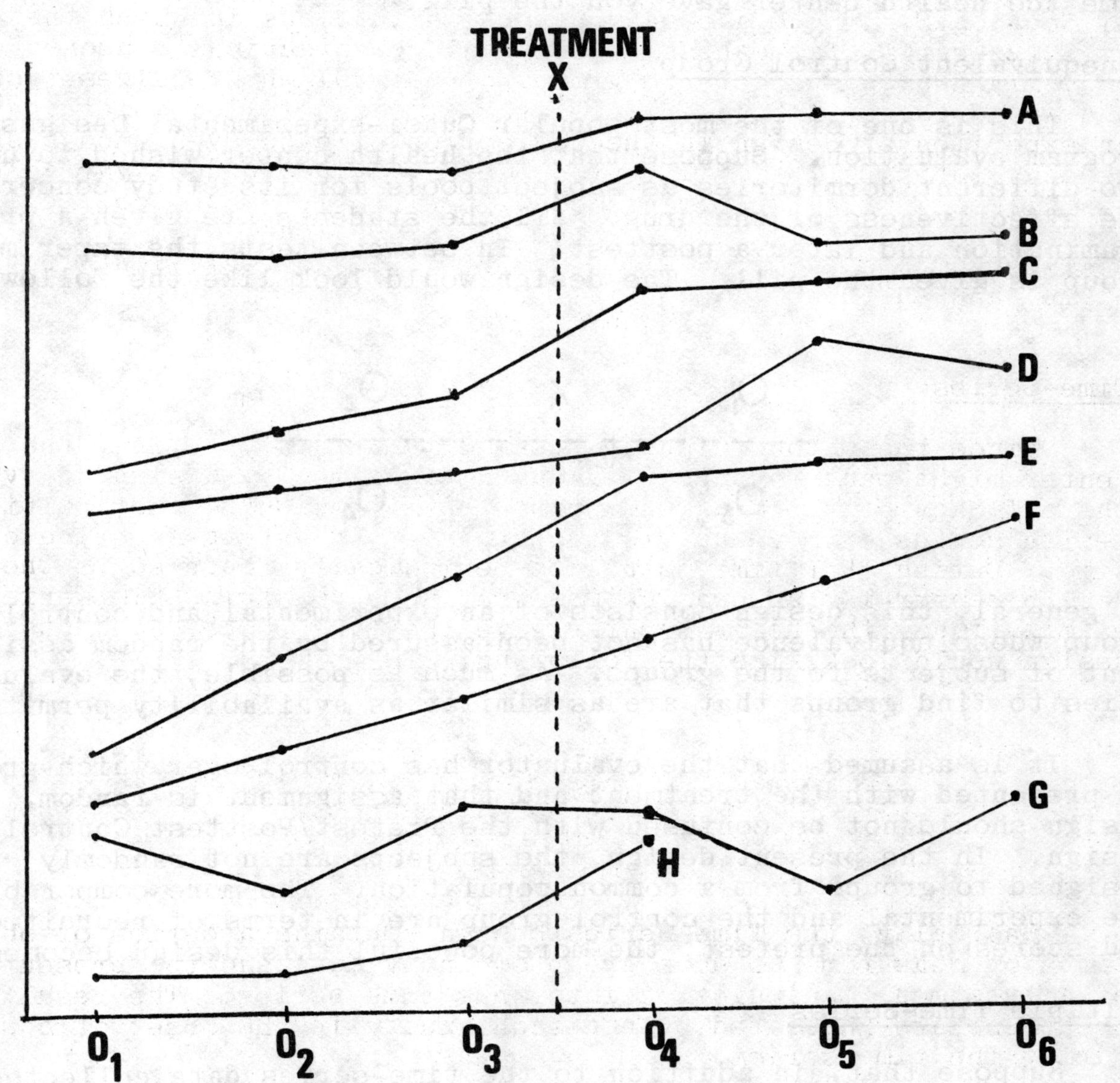

*Adapted from Campbell and Stanley (1963).

the change in the dependent variable, you increase the strength of the inferences made from the experimental results. As was noted in the One-Group Pretest/Posttest, this design is susceptible to the confounding influences of a sunny day which might occur at the same time the health center gave you the pill.

Nonequivalent Control Group

This is one of the most popular Quasi-experimental Designs for program evaluation. Suppose that the health center wished to use two different dormitories as subject pools for its study concerning the effectiveness of the drug. All the students are given a pretest examination and later a posttest. In between tests the experimental group is given the pill. The design would look like the following:

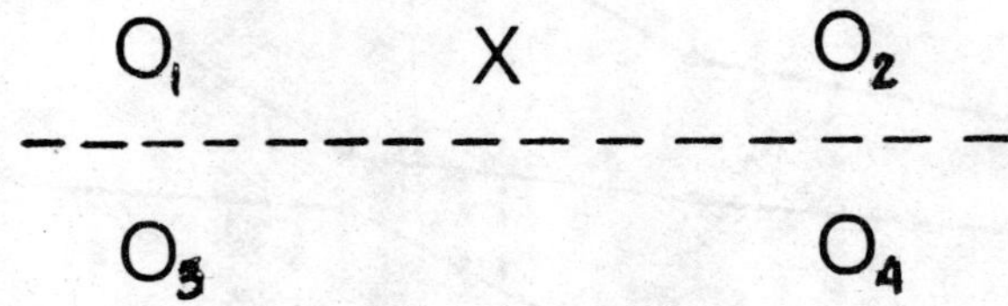

In general, this design consists of an experimental and control group whose equivalence has not been assured by the random assignment of subjects to the groups. As much as possible, the evaluator tries to find groups that are as similar as availability permits.

It is assumed that the evaluator has control over which group is presented with the treatment and that assignment is random. This design should not be confused with the Pretest/Posttest Control Group Design. In the present design, the subjects are <u>not</u> randomly assigned to groups from a common population. The more comparable the experimental and the control group are in terms of recruitment and scores on the pretest, the more powerful this design becomes.

Multiple Time-Series

Suppose that, in addition to the time-series data collected for the previous design, the health center corresponded with another university health center and asked it to collect a similar time series without the treatment, X, being presented. The basic design could be diagrammed as follows:

$$O_1 O_2 O_3 O_4 X O_5 O_6 O_7 O_8$$
$$O_9 O_{10} O_{11} O_{12} O_{13} O_{14} O_{15} O_{16}$$

In essence, this design is a combination of the Nonequivalent Control
Group Design and the Time-Series Design. In most evaluations of this
type, evaluators obtain their data from a similar institution which
is not exposed to the treatment.

The design contains within it the strengths of the two previous
Quasi-experimental Designs. In addition, any change in the dependent
variable caused by the treatment is confirmed twice, first against
the control group and second against its own pre-X observations.

Quasi-experimental Designs: Conclusions

The Multiple Time-Series Design is the best and most highly
recommended of the Quasi-experimental Designs. While all the designs
have certain weaknesses, they should be used for program evaluation
where circumstances preclude the use of the stronger True-experimental
Designs.

EXERCISE 5.4: Identifying Designs

Under each of the three sections below -- Pre-experimental
Designs, True-experimental Designs, and Quasi-experimental Designs
-- read the four brief evaluation statements and determine which of
the designs best describes the approach of the evaluator. Identify
the various components of the evaluation using the Campbell and
Stanley notation in justifying your description.

Part 1. Pre-experimental Designs

1. A countywide campaign against child abuse is carried out over
    a period of six months. At the completion of the campaign,
    the county supervisors compare the rate of child abuse in their
    county with the rate for the neighboring county. On the basis
    of that comparison, they conclude that the campaign was a success.

2. A Federal agency observes that the crime rate is increasing.
   It supplies the local law enforcement departments with massive
   amounts of Federal aid. A year later the agency notes that the
   increase in the crime rate is less than the previous year. The
   agency concludes that massive aid to local police departments
   helped decrease the rate of crime in the country.

3. An after-school program to increase the reading level of minority
   students is begun. At the end of the school year, the reading
   level of the children in the program is lower than the rest of
   the children in the school. The principal concludes that the
   program was a waste of money and resources.

4. A local city council is concerned about the number of bicycle
    thefts which have occurred. It institutes a program to get
    everyone to lock their bicycles. One month after the program
    the number of bicycles stolen is reduced. The city council
    concludes that the program was a success.

Part 2. True-experimental Designs

1. A local city council is concerned about drug use among teen-
    agers in the city. The council wants to know if live speak-
    ers are effective in changing the teenagers' attitude toward
    drugs. It is also interested in finding out if this pre-
    sentation is more effective than no presentation at all. All
    the local high school students are tested about their attitude
    toward drugs. They are then randomly assigned to one of the
    two conditions outlined above. After being exposed to one of
    the two conditions, all the students are again tested about
    their attitude toward drugs.

2. A local police department is interested in finding out if role-playing is an effective method for teaching crisis intervention techniques. Police officers are randomly assigned to one of two conditions. One group uses role-playing techniques and then is tested. A second group receives no additional train- and is just tested.

3. Patients in a mental hospital are randomly assigned to one of the following conditions. In the first group, the patients' social interaction in the dining room is observed at the beginning of the month. They are then given a therapy program designed to increase their social interaction. At the end of the month, their behavior in the dining room is observed again. In the second group, the patients are given the same therapy program as the first group. At the end of the month, they too are observed in the dining room. The third group is observed in the dining room at the beginning and at the end of the month. The fourth group of patients is observed in the dining room at the end of the month.

4. A local high school is interested in evaluating a new slide-
   tape program concerning driver education. The students are
   randomly assigned to one of two conditions. In the first condition, the students do not see the slide-tape show. The
   second group watches the slide-tape presentation. After the
   slide-tape presentation, all of the students are given a
   questionnaire concerning driver education.

Part 3. Quasi-experimental Designs

1. Children at two different day-care centers are tested for their
   verbal abilities. After the test, a program designed to improve verbal skills is begun at one of the centers. At the
   completion of the program, the children in both centers are
   tested again.

2. State legislators, concerned over the yearly increase in traffic deaths during the previous five years, passed a 55 m.p.h. speed limit. During the four years after the law was passed, the yearly increases were reduced. The legislators conclude that the 55 m.p.h. speed limit was responsible for the change in traffic fatalities.

3. The county police department has noticed an increase in the number of arrests for driving while intoxicated during the past three years. They conduct a three-month program aimed at reducing the number of drunk drivers on the road. For three years after the program, they collect data on the number of drunk drivers arrested in the county. At the end of the second three-year period, they compare the number of drunken drivers arrested during all of the preceding six years with the yearly arrests of drunk drivers for the same six-year period in a neighboring county.

4. A university library is concerned about the number of books which have been stolen in each of the past four semesters. The library personnel develop new checking-out procedures. The number of stolen books is recorded each semester for the next three semesters. At the end of the third semester, the number of stolen books has been reduced. The library administration concludes that the program was a success.

EXERCISE 5.5: Research Designs

Part 1. What research design will you use? Discuss the diagram associated with the design. Be specific about the source and method of data collection.

Part 2. Why did you select this design over the others? Discuss this with respect to monetary costs, feasibility, availability of information, and length of time of study.

V: THE QUESTION OF VALIDITY

After you have selected the proper design, collected the data, and reached a conclusion about whether or not the program had the intended effect, you still need to address the question of the validity of the results. By validity, we mean whether or not your findings are "true." Millions of words have been written about the nature and meaning of truth, and it is impossible in this section to deal with the serious philosophical problems associated with the question "how do we know truth." However, it is possible to look at a study and identify the considerations that might render a particular result untrue. In the social sciences, we never determine truth definitively. We merely eliminate as much as possible the factors that might bias the results of our findings.

The chart below presents a starting point in assessing the validity of findings that might come from a given study. On the columns we ask the question "did the study find the program successful," and on the rows we ask the question "was the program really successful." When you are in the process of designing the study, analyzing the information, and reaching conclusions, you need to keep in mind the two questions posed by the lower left-hand and upper right-hand boxes. These are:

1. If my data show that the program was successful, what factors could have shaped the data even though the program was not in reality successful?

2. If my data show that the program was unsuccessful, what factors would have shaped the data even though the program really did have the intended effect?

Considering Factors That Render Program Evaluations Invalid:
Results of Study

		Program Works	Program Does Not Work
Reality	Program Works	Valid	Invalid
	Program Does Not Work	Invalid	Valid

To illustrate how you might take into consideration questions 1 and 2, let us assume you are studying the implementation of a curfew on the drinking of alcoholic beverages at parties in a university dormitory. If you conducted a study and found less vandalism attributable to drunkenness after the policy was implemented than before, you might conclude that the policy worked. However, you would need to deal with such questions as did the general level of drinking among college-level age groups decline after the policy was implemented; did the amount of vandalism outside the dormitories (that is, in the local bars) increase; did the price of alcoholic beverages increase; did the weather get better so that students could play outside more than they could prior to the implementation of the policy; or did the policy itself not have the impact, but the publicity given to alcoholism and vandalism stimulated by the policy make the difference.

Similarly, if the study showed that vandalism due to alcoholism did not decrease (either stayed the same or increased), the conclusion that the policy did not work would not necessarily be valid. Such factors as an increase in the number of rowdy alcoholic students on campus, the relative inexpensiveness of alcohol as a form of entertainment (it's almost cheaper than ice cream), the increase in the number of students in dorms, the reduction of the supply of drugs, or reduction in the number of bars in the university areas could have caused an increase in alcohol-inspired vandalism in the dorms. The program may have had the effect of not allowing these factors to increase alcohol-inspired vandalism but the findings would indicate the policy was a failure.

All of these factors could render your conclusions invalid, and it is impossible to eliminate the effect of all of them on your findings. What you need to do is to recognize that they exist, construct your research design so that as many of these factors are controlled for in one way or another, and identify the problems when you write up your results. On top of these considerations, we need also to point out that the data themselves may not represent what they are supposed to. In many cases, how you measure the effect of the policy is open to debate. In our university alcohol policy illustration, for example, how information is collected on the amount of alcohol-inspired vandalism could seriously affect the results of the study. Those keeping the records could over-report the amount of vandalism depending on whether or not they support the policy. The procedures for determing whether or not vandalism is caused by individuals under the influence of alcohol is open to question. If the total amount of vandalism -- rather than that inspired by alcohol -- is used, the amount of vandalism could increase or decrease irrespective of the use of alcohol.

The question of validity, then, is clearly essential to consider in designing a program evaluation and reporting its conclusion. While

it is impossible to reach a firm conclusion that a given finding is
valid, the research must always seek to reduce as much as possible
the source of factors that render the study invalid. To ignore
these sources is to produce a study of little use.

EXERCISE 5.6: <u>Validity</u>

Discuss how the study might have produced positive results for
reasons other than that the program had worked. Discuss how the
design might have produced negative results for reasons other than
that the program did not work. Discuss how your data may not represent what they are supposed to.

CHAPTER SIX: ANALYZING POLITICS WITH THE PRINCE
POLITICAL ACCOUNTING SYSTEM

THE PRIMARY OBJECTIVE:

This chapter is an introduction to the PRINCE Political Accounting System.

UPON COMPLETION OF THIS CHAPTER, YOU WILL BE ABLE TO:

* Identify the actors involved in the formulation and implementation of a given public policy

* Gather information on the factors shaping the behavior of the actors toward that issue

* Interpret those factors through the PRINCE Political Accounting System so that alternative political strategies can be assessed.

(For a booklength discussion of the PRINCE System see: William D. Coplin and Michael K. O'Leary, Everyman's PRINCE: A Guide to Understanding Your Political Problems. 2nd ed., North Scituate, MA: Duxbury Press, 1976.

I: INTRODUCTION

The PRINCE Political Accounting System is a technique for assessing the impact of various individuals, groups, and organizations on public policy decisions. The basic assumption behind the PRINCE System is that in order to assess the impact of relevant individuals, groups, and organizations on any decision, it is necessary to do the following:

- Identify the individuals, groups, and organizations (the "actors") that are likely to have a direct or indirect impact on the decision. This includes those that have a formal role in the making or blocking of the decision. It also means including those who have an indirect impact -- those making it either easier or harder to carry out a decision after it is made.

- Determing whether each actor supports, opposes, or is neutral toward the decision. (This is called "issue position.")

- Determine how effective each actor is in blocking the decision, helping make it happen, or effecting the implementation of a decision. (This is called "power.")

- Determine how important the decision is to each actor. (This is called "salience.")

When making decisions, key individuals -- the President, a legislator, a regional governmental official, a business executive, a school superintendent, or the head of the household -- always perform these kinds of analyses, if only informally. The purpose of the PRINCE System is to provide a systematic framework and checklist which decision makers can use to make sure they carry out the kind of analysis required to assess the consequences of a decision. The PRINCE System also aids decision makers in organizing their staffs and making use of knowledgeable observers.

II. STEPS IN COMPLETING THE PRINCE SYSTEM

The basic steps followed in completing the PRINCE System are
shown below:

Step 1: Define the Issue

An issue is a proposed decision or action which is likely to
generate controversy. It may be a local ordinance, a national policy
decision, or an international foreign policy issue. The PRINCE
System can be applied when the proposed decision is clearly defined
in specific terms, in a phrase beginning with a verb. If an issue
is defined as "protecting the environment" or "improving the
efficiency of an agency's regulatory procedure," it would not be
possible to complete a PRINCE Analysis. But the analysis can be
done on specific issues such as "issue a general regulation controlling the landfill activities of private landowners." The key is
found in the verb used to phrase the decision. Verbs such as "pro-
tect" or "improve" are undesirable because they do not adequately
specify the required action. Verbs like "restrict," "vote,"
"oppose," "permit," or "build" are much more useful.

While decisions or actions need to be specifically defined in
order to conduct analysis, trying to guess at the exact detail of
the final formulation is not required. One of the main characteristics of reaching decisions affecting many actors is that the action
is frequently redefined and modified as a result of the process of
reaching a decision. The decision may begin as "issue a general
regulation that governs landfill activities of private landowners"
and become modified to "issue a general regulation that governs landfill activities of private landowners _and_ commercial property under
a certain acreage." Such a change may be required to obtain the
support of important groups to solve technical problems in adminis-
tering the permit. The PRINCE System can be applied to any number
of proposed decisions (including redefinitions and modifications) as
long as it is clear _what_ specific action is involved at each point
along the way.

Another important consideration in picking a decision is to make
sure that there is both significant support and opposition. It is

pointless to analyze a decision that is either so well accepted or
so widely opposed that the outcome is obvious. Of course, few
decisions affecting the public result in overwhelming support or
opposition. However, when they do come along they do not need to
be analyzed systematically.

Step 2: Identify Actors

An actor is any individual, group, or organization that ought
to be considered in making the decision or in carrying it out after
it has been made. Reasons for including an actor are any of the
following: The actor has substantial legal authority; the actor has
political influence to promote or obstruct the decision; or the
actor will be seriously affected by the decision and may either help
or hinder its implementation, even though it may not have much of a
say in the actual making of the decision.

Identifying the actors to be considered is one of the most
important steps in the PRINCE System. Omitting an important actor
or incorrectly grouping actors can distort the analysis so much that
the analysis becomes useless.

In order to keep the analysis within feasible bounds, limit the
number of actors to 20 -- or even less, if possible. In situations
where time is short, try to limit the number of actors to 10 or less.
The reason for limiting the number of actors is to limit the time
required for listing and calculations required for the PRINCE
System.

The principal way to limit the number of actors is to group
individuals and organizations into collective actors for the purpose
of analysis. The process of grouping frequently appears arbitrary
and, as mentioned earlier, can seriously bias your results if it is
not done carefully. However, there are some guidelines that will
assist you in grouping actors to help improve the accuracy of your
analysis:

.   Group actors together that have the same economic
    interests. In dealing with an environmental issue,
    for example, all private developers might be grouped
    together for this reason.

.   Do not group together actors that have veto power.
    This especially holds for governmental actors. For
    example, the U.S. Fish and Wildlife Service might be
    kept separate from the Environmental Protection Agency,
    but similar State Agencies (Natural Resources and
    Environmental Regulation) could be combined.

- <u>Do not</u> group together actors if there is disagreement among them or if their components have widely unequal power. For example, a city government could be combined as a single actor if there were general agreement among all members of the government concerning the issue and if each person in the governing unit had approximately equal power. If there were disagreements, or if some members were much more powerful than others, it would be preferable to divide them into two (or more) actors.

- Select a configuration of actors that taken together constitute a reasonable picture of the overall power distribution. <u>Do not</u> include an excess of actors that gives one side an unrealistic weighting. If there is one collective actor with an immense amount of power, that actor should be divided into enough smaller actors so that the total power configuration is accurately reflected.

These guidelines are admittedly quite general. The designation of the actors in the PRINCE System is at least as much an art as a science. Your judgment in conducting the analysis is vital at every step. In one sense, this might be viewed as a weakness in the technique, but not really. The system is a way of organizing and guiding judgment, not eliminating it. It would be foolish to ignore the importance of judgment and balanced insight (even if it were possible to do so) in the selection of actors as well as in the other aspects of PRINCE analysis.

<u>Step 3: Estimate Issue Position, Power, and Salience for Each Actor</u>
        (See Table 6.1)

<u>Issue Position</u> is the current general attitude of the actor toward the decision. It is expressed as a number ranging from +3 to -3 to indicate whether or not the actor supports (+3, +2, or +1), is neutral toward (0), or opposes (-1, -2, or -3) the decision. A "+3" is assigned if the actor is firmly in favor of the issue and is unlikely to change; "+2" or "+1" indicates reduced levels of firmness of the actors support. Similarly, a "-3" indicates firm opposition while a "-2" or "-1" indicates there is some softness in the opposition.

<u>Power</u> is defined as the degree to which the actor can exert influence, directly or indirectly, in support of or in opposition to the decision, relative to all other actors. The basis of an actor's power as well as the ways in which this power may be exercised are varied. Power may be based on such factors as group size, wealth, physical resources, institutional authority, prestige, and

TABLE 6.1: PRINCE Chart

(State in terms of a desired political outcome using a phrase beginning with a verb.)

ACTORS	ISSUE POSITION	X	POWER	X	SALIENCE	=	TOTAL SUPPORT BY ACTOR
	-3-0-+3		1-3		1-3		
		X		X		=	
		X		X		=	
		X		X		=	
		X		X		=	
		X		X		=	
		X		X		=	
		X		X		=	
		X		X		=	

political skill. Power is expressed as a number ranging from 1 to
3. A "1" is assigned if the actor has a slight amount of power; a
"2" if the actor has moderate power. A "3" is assigned if an actor
has substantial influence, especially if the actor can veto or pre-
vent the implementation of the decision.

<u>Salience</u> is defined as the importance the actor attaches to
supporting or opposing the decision relative to all other decisions
with which that actor is concerned. Salience is expressed as a
number ranging from 1 to 3. A "1" indicates slight interest or concern for the issue regardless of the issue position or power. A
"2" is assigned for those actors that have moderate concern. A "3"
is reversed for those actors that assign the highest priority to the
issue.

The task of estimating each actor's issue position, power, and
salience can be facilitated by the following suggestions.

When estimating an actor's issue position:

- Read and listen to what the actor says about the
  issue.

- Deduce from the actor's economic, social, or political
  standing what its position is likely to be on the
  basis of self-interest.

- Weigh the implications of concrete interests against
  what it has said. When in doubt, use concrete
  interests for your estimate over mere verbalizations.

- Look for differences among individuals and factions
  within a collective actor. Look for inconsistencies
  in statements by an individual actor. If the contrasting positions seem evenly balanced, assign a "0"
  (neutral) issue position. If there seems a slight
  positive or negative balance toward the issue, assign
  a "+1" or "-1" for the actor's issue position.

When estimating an actor's <u>power</u>:

- Ask if the actor has the resources either to block a
  decision or to make one occur.

- Determine if legal authority is a consideration and
  if the actor possesses a large share of the authority.

- Consider whether an actor has the ability to help or
  hinder the carrying out of a decision. (This is why
  constituency groups have power.)

. Determine, if wealth is a consideration, how much wealth
  the actor has.

. Do not assume that an actor powerful on one set of issues
  is necessarily powerful on all issues. It is true that
  an actor's high power on one issue means it _may_ have power
  on other issues, but it does not assure high power.

. Consider the allies and enemies of the actor. Powerful
  allies makes the actor powerful; powerful enemies diminish
  the actor's power.

When estimating _salience_:

. Determine the frequency and intensity with which the actor
  makes public statements about the decision.

. Deduce from the actor's social, political, and economic
  interests the importance it is likely to attach to the
  decision.

. Watch out for the fact that salience can be rapidly and
  substantially altered by external events and the intru-
  sion of other issues.

. Remember that other decisions and factors compete for the
  actor's attention and, hence, its salience.

Like selecting actors, the assignment of issue position, power, and
salience is something of an art. Systematic research can play an
important role, but the importance of the skillful assessment of
existing conditions by knowledgeable and sensible observers is abso-
lutely essential. Therefore, it is important that those completing
the charts be thoroughly familiar with the situation. They should
talk to other knowledgeable people and gather all available information on the reactions of individuals, groups, and organizations to
the proposed decision.

Step 4: Calculate the Weights for Each Actor and for the Whole System

     After the estimates are made for each actor, the next step is
to calculate the weights each actor contributes in the decision. This
is done by multiplying issue position times power times salience for
each actor. Issue position (alone of the three variables) may be
either positive or negative. (The other two are always positive.)
Therefore, the sign of the issue position will be the sign of the
weight for each actor. After each actor's weight is calculated,
determine the overall sum by adding the signed numbers. (See Table
6.2.)

<u>Step 5: Calculating Probabilities</u>

By completing the following steps, the weights calculated for each actor can also be used to estimate the probability of the decision's being adopted.

1. Add together the scores of all the actors supporting the decision. Call this total "A."

2. Add together the scores of all the actors opposing the issue. Eliminate the minus sign. (This is called taking the "absolute value" of the number.) Call this total "B."

3. Multiply the nonzero scores of all the actors that have a neutral issue position, and add together these scores. Call this total "C."

4. Add together "A," "B," and "C." This is the total of all the power weights in the particular system as you have described it with your PRINCE analysis. Call this total "D."

5. Add together "A" and <u>one-half</u> the value of "C," the neutral actors' scores. Call this total "E." The reason for including one-half the value of "C" is that the neutral actors are equally likely, in the future, to be either supporters or opponents of the issue. The best way to represent this 50-50 situation in the absence of other information is to include just half of the neutral actors' scores with the positive weights. Total "E" is the sum of the best estimate of the likely weights to be exerted in support of the issue.

6. Divide "E" (the weights supporting the issue) by "D" (the total weights in the system.) The resulting fraction is proportion of positive weights in relation to the total weights. It can be interpreted as the likelihood that the issue will be supported -- that the decision, law, or whatever is represented by the issue, will be implemented. This fraction, like all probability numbers, ranges from 0.0 (no chance of occurrence) to 1.00 (certainty of occurrence). These numbers are frequently reported as 0% to 100%. Note that if the probability is low, this may mean two things: either the decision will be defeated, or it will continue as a controversial issue without being decided one way or another. The closer the supporting and opposing weights are to each other, the more likely the issue will continue as a controversial topic without being resolved one way or another.

Table 6.2 has a completed PRINCE chart on the issue of maintaining present tuition rates for the next academic year at a university.

TABLE 6.2: PRINCE Chart

ISSUE: Maintain the Same Tuition Cost from 1980-81 to 1981-82

(State in terms of a desired political outcome
using a phrase beginning with a verb.)

ACTORS	ISSUE POSITION	X	POWER	X	SALIENCE	=	TOTAL SUPPORT BY ACTOR
	-3-0-+3		1-3		1-3		
Administration	-2	X	3	X	3	=	-18
Board of Trustees	0	X	2	X	2	=	(4)
SA/Students in Senate	+3	X	1	X	2	=	+ 6
Faculty in Senate	-2	X	3	X	2	=	-12
Parents Office	+2	X	2	X	1	=	+ 4
Budget Committee	-2	X	1	X	3	=	- 6

Totals: A - Scores of all actors supporting the issue: <u>10</u>
B - Absolute value of actors opposing the issue: <u>36</u>
C - Scores of actors with zero issue positions: <u>4</u>
D - Totals A, B, C: <u>50</u>
E - Total A + 1/2 of Total C: <u>12</u>
Probability of Support = $\frac{E}{D} = \frac{12}{50} = .24$ (24%)

Note that the students and the representatives of the parents are in favor of maintaining the present levels. They have a weight of 10; this is total "A." The administration, the general faculty, and the faculty senate budget committee are opposed. Their scores, total "B," have an absolute value of 36. And the board of trustees is neutral; their score, total "C," is 4. The total scores of all the actors (counting the product of the nonzero scores for the board of trustees) is 50. The total of these in favor of holding the line on tuition is 10; to this is added 2 points (one-half of the score of the neutral board of trustees) for a total of 12, total "E." The basic PRINCE calculation, then, is "E" divided by "D," 12/50, or only .24 -- also expressed as a 24% chance that the present tuition rate will remain the same for the forthcoming academic year. In other words, this forecast indicates the chances are quite small that the rates will remain the same.

You should note that this analysis could have been prepared by having the issue states as "Raise tuition rates for the forthcoming year." In this case, the signs of the issue positions would be reversed. The resulting calculations would have been based on a total of 36 points for those supporting an increase, plus 2 points for the neutral board of trustees, for a total of 38 divided by 50, for a probability of 76% that the increase would take place. Saying that there is only a 24% chance that no increase will occur is the same as saying that there is a 76% chance that an increase will occur. (Incidently, the increase did occur, confirming the unhappy prediction.) It is a matter of convenience whether the issue is stated as affirmatively, making an action occur, or negatively, preventing an action from occurring.

EXERCISE 6.1: Conducting a PRINCE Analysis

Identify a public policy -- either one existing or one proposed -- and conduct a PRINCE Analysis to determine whether or not
the policy will continue (if it already exists) or will be implemented (if it is proposed). Complete each of the first five steps
outlined in this section on the PRINCE chart below.

(State in terms of a desired political outcome
using a phrase beginning with a verb.)

ACTORS	ISSUE POSITION	X	POWER	X	SALIENCE	=	TOTAL SUPPORT BY ACTOR
	-3-0-+3		1-3		1-3		
		X		X		=	
		X		X		=	
		X		X		=	
		X		X		=	
		X		X		=	
		X		X		=	
		X		X		=	
		X		X		=	

Totals: A - Scores of all actors supporting the issue: __
         B - Absolute value of actors opposing the issue: __
         C - Scores of actors with zero issue positions: __
         D - Totals A, B, C: __
         E - Total A + 1/2 of Total C: __
         Probability of Support = $\frac{E}{D}$ = __________

Step 6: Strategies

One of the prime values of the PRINCE Political Accounting System is that it enables you to formulate on a systematic basis strategies that you might want to pursue to achieve a political outcome. In order to use the system, the first thing that you must decide is what political outcome you would like to achieve. In terms of the probability estimate generated by your analysis, do you want a higher or lower probability? Once you have decided that question, you need to take the role of one of the actors in the PRINCE chart or to take a role that you can visualize would allow you to influence actors in the PRINCE chart.

After making a decision on what your political goal is and whom you will represent, you can explore strategies under the following principles:

1. Formulate your decision so that you get the most important components of what you want, while making potential opposition actors as happy as possible.

2. Try to stimulate actors who are not on the PRINCE chart to become interested or powerful enough to warrant placing them on the PRINCE chart.

3. Change issue position of actors so that they agree with you, or if they already agree with you, more firmly agree with you. This can be done by:

   a) Using arguments of a symbolic or factual kind
   b) Making promises
   c) Making threats
   d) Establishing friendly relations with or becoming
       enemies of those who are the enemies of the actors
       whose issue positions you wish to change.

4. Change power of yourself and those who support you relative to those who do not support your position by:

   a) Gaining wealth
   b) Improving your organization to deliver votes, money,
       or other expressions of support (e.g., letters to
       Congressmen)
   c) Acquiring knowledge and expertise
   d) Making friends
   e) Isolating enemies.

5. Change salience of yourself and those who support you relative to those who do not support your position by:

a) Raising salience:

    i) Create an event that generates publicity
   ii) Distribute information about the issue.

b) Lowering salience:

    i) Keep issue out of the press or other publicity
      media
   ii) Raise another issue that deflects attention of
      actors whose salience you wish to lower.

EXERCISE 6.2: Using Strategies

Choose the role of one of the actors from the PRINCE chart completed in Exercise 6.1 and develop two strategies to raise the probability of your desired outcome.